Marketing for the HOME-BASED BUSINESS

SECOND EDITION

Marketing for the HOME-BASED BUSINESS

SECOND EDITION

JEFF DAVIDSON, MBA CMC

Adams Media Corporation
Holbrook, Massachusetts

Published by
Adams Media Corporation
260 Center Street, Holbrook, MA 02343

ISBN: 1-58062-078-7

Printed in the United States of America.
J I H G F E D C B A

Library of Congress Cataloging-in-Publication Data
Davidson, Jeffrey P.
Marketing for the home-based business / by Jeff Davidson.
p. cm.
ISBN 1-58062-078-7
1. Home-based businesses—United States. I. Title.
HD2333.D39   1999
658'.041—dc21   98-26818
CIP

This publication is designed to provide accurate and authoritative information
with regard to the subject matter covered. It is sold with the understanding that
the publisher is not engaged in rendering legal, accounting, or other professional
advice. If legal advice or other expert assistance is required, the services of a
competent professional person should be sought.
— From a *Declaration of Principles* jointly adopted by a Committee of the
American Bar Association and a Committee of Publishers and Associations

This book is available at quantity discounts for bulk purchases.
For information, call 1-800-872-5627
(in Massachusetts, 781-767-8100).

Visit our home page at http://www.adamsmedia.com

TABLE OF CONTENTS

ACKNOWLEDGMENTS

No one operates a business alone—not when you consider suppliers, creditors, and customers, not to mention family or housemates, counselors and friends. Similarly, no one writes a book alone. In the course of writing this book and more than two dozen others, I have benefitted from the contributions of countless subject matter experts, cronies, and sounding boards: among them David Arnold, Ph.D, Ron Wagner, Richard Connor, Stewart Crump, Guy Kawasaki, Martin Edelston, Tony Alessandra, Ph.D, Rebecca Morgan, Karen Stelmach, Al Reis, Jack Trout, Jim Cathcart, Bill Brooks, Alvin Toffler, Dave Yoho, Robert Cialdini, Ph.D., Edie Fraser, and Catherine Fyock.

Also Margaret Hickey, Peter Hicks, Marilyn Leibrenz Himes, Ph.D., Bob Scarlata, Marty Horn, Richard Levy, Vicki Lovett, Patricia Fripp, Alan Schlaifer, and Chris Klose. Special thanks to Katy Crowthers, Jennifer Springs, Anna Mayes, Seth Kotch, Kate Simpson for their crackerjack proofreading.

Thanks also to Bob Adams for his unwavering vision, Ed Walters, Wayne Jackson, Nancy True, and Carrie Lewis.

Foreword

The explosive growth of home-based businesses across America and throughout the world is one of the most exciting developments of the late twentieth and early twenty-first century. With this development comes the potential for renewed strength of the family, of communities, and greater financial well-being for more people.

The home-based business phenomena in America is not new. Prior to World War II, most people maintained a home-based business in one form or another. The farmer set up an office in the kitchen, on the dining room table, or in the spare room in the back of the house. Often, the entrepreneurial merchant lived upstairs or right next to his establishment. Long before the Kmarts and Wal-Marts of the world, the mom and pop grocery store, the five-and-dime department store, and the corner service station flourished.

Today, as one spectacular technological breakthrough after another occurs, home-based business entrepreneurs have the means to be more effective working from home than one could have even imagined twenty years ago. As you're about to see in *Marketing for the Home-Based Business*, the opportunity to market your home-based business effectively is limited only by your imagination. As Jeff Davidson shows you in chapter after chapter, regardless of the size of your office, the nature of your business, and the resources you have at hand, you have many options when it comes to marketing your business effectively.

Jeff explains how to use the telephone to its full advantage. you'll learn how to use the Internet to make money; how to leverage your professional relationships, why it's so important to use part-time help, and dozens of other profit building ideas. I am a home-based business entrepreneur myself, operating a virtual office. I have nearly two dozen employees and contacts worldwide.

I continually stay in touch by phone, fax, and modem. These ideas really work!

Marketing for the Home-Based Business is a practical, down-to-earth, "here's how you do it" guidebook. It speaks to you in straightforward, everyday language. Jeff's writing style makes it seem as if he's speaking to you as a friend, right across the table from you. He often anticipates that question you want to ask. The suggestions he offers are both easy to understand and easy to follow.

Whether you've just launched a home-based venture or have been in business for years, you'll find this book to be just what the doctor ordered, if your goal is to effectively market your home-based business, not pay a fortune in doing so, and still have a home life. Use this book to rearrange your office or your whole orientation to marketing. Refer to it again and again for the ideas and insights presented on each page. Continually delve into it to inspire yourself to action and to propel your business forward.

There has never been a better time to be in business for yourself and to be working out of your home. With this valuable guidebook, you will save a lot of time and money in getting up to speed and moving toward financial independence.

Brian Tracy, CPAE, author of *Maximum Achievement*
Solana Beach, CA
January, 1999

Introduction

There has never been a better time to be in business for yourself, operating from home, than right now.

In his landmark and now apocalyptic book, *Future Shock* (1969), Alvin Toffler described the rise of the cottage industry. He foresaw a nation and a world dotted with entrepreneurs operating with high-technology equipment in a low-cost environment—their homes. Now, three decades since Toffler's vision, the home-based business is a burgeoning phenomenon. Articles in *Time, Newsweek, The Economist, U. S. News and World Report, Changing Times, Fast Forward, Business Week, Forbes, Fortune, Nation's Business, Money, Worth, Success,* and *Modern Maturity,* as well as the *New York Times, Los Angeles Times, Chicago Tribune, Wall Street Journal, Washington Post,* and virtually every other newspaper available have heralded and chronicled its development.

Amazingly, with every tick of the clock something happens in the world that potentially facilitates your ability to market more effectively, if not flourish, in a home-based business. Professor Lowell Catlett, noted author and professor at New Mexico State University, says that the rate of change in the United States and Canada is such that there's a new high-technology product in the marketplace every 17 seconds. That's more than 3 a minute, more than 200 an hour, and well more than 5,000 a day. With each new high-technology product comes at least one hundred related services. Yet, in a handful of years there will be 17 new high-technology products produced every second!

Despite the potential for confusion and the array of options that the home-based entrepreneur faces, *the basics of successfully marketing from home remain surprising simple.*

This book addresses marketing strategies that you can use to succeed in marketing your home-based business. It focuses on fundamental methods and approaches for using available resources to assist you in the most crucial aspect of operating your own business: *marketing*.

If you're like most home-based entrepreneurs, among your goals in operating a home-based business and successfully marketing it are:

- To market effectively without spending a fortune
- To maintain a professional image
- To protect and preserve your home life
- To avoid common marketing pitfalls

This book will help you market your service or product to appropriate targets from an office (or other facilities) within your home. This book is for you, if you:

- Already have a home office and would like to be more effective at marketing your business
- Will soon start a home-based business
- Have a job, either full- or part-time, outside the home while also maintaining a home office
- Operate a small or one-person business outside the home but frequently handle marketing tasks at home
- Want to be more effective at marketing with no staff or limited help
- Are undecided as to what you want to do but are interested in strategies for marketing from home

What This Book Is Not

This book is not the be-all and end-all text on marketing, small business marketing, cyber-marketing, or operating a home-based business in general. Rather, it is a distinct view of *key factors that impact a home-based entrepreneur's ability to market effectively from home*. This makes it unique from other books.

As with all business decisions, the marketing strategies discussed all have their advantages and disadvantages, and this book frequently summarizes the pros and cons of strategies following their explanation. I will assume from the outset that you already possess and use an e-mail address. Possibly, you even have a business Web site. I will not, however, delve into the technical aspects of established or emerging software or hardware; there are plenty of articles about that, that will keep you far more current than any book can. Similarly, direct mail, catalog sales, and selling in general will not be addressed here.

I will discuss fundamental strategies and techniques upon which you can rely to support your marketing efforts that are attuned to the special needs and challenges of home-based entrepreneurs. Let's begin by reaffirming that the environment for starting and successfully marketing a home-based business has never been more favorable than it is right now!

CHAPTER 1

Setting Up at Home

*The sweetest commute in the world is that 8-second
walk from your bedroom to your home office.*

So many millions of people are operating home-based businesses today that it is changing the nature of society. When you boil down everything that has happened that impacts the home-business boom, four factors emerge:

- An explosion in information technology
- Economic insecurity
- Changing demographics
- Restructured families

An Explosion in Information Technology

By some estimates, at least 42 million Americans now opt to commute to another room of the house either full- or part-time to work for themselves or others. Slightly more than one out of three new businesses in the United States is run out of the home. Meanwhile, the home-based business phenomenon is in full swing in other Western or industrialized nations.

More than 60% of U. S. home offices have a PC. Link Resources, a research leader regarding the home-based business phenomena, estimates that the sales of products and services for the home office will top $15 billion. The Yankee Group predicts 50%

of all U. S. homes will have more than one telephone line within 5 years, fueled by the purchase of home fax machines and fax/modems.

A visit to any office superstore readily reveals that PCs with built-in modems and CD-ROM drives, color printers, personal copiers, fax machines, color scanners, answering machines, and multifunction telephones, are all affordable and easier to use than ever before.

What's even more amazing is that so many people learned to use PCs at all! Alvin Toffler notes that at least 60 million people in the United States alone have learned to use the personal computer since its mass introduction in 1980. This learning came about without a formal plan and without formal education; most users did not attend classes of any kind. They learned from mentors and friends, when and where they could.

Clearly, Toffler says, something happened on an individual basis, resulting in mass change. Before it became comfortable and familiar to them, many home-based PC users spent hours learning word processing, spreadsheet, and database programs.

The "electronic cottage" is reverting America back to an employment pattern common at the turn of the nineteenth century. Most Americans worked for themselves back then; they were family farmers, shopkeepers, and small manufacturers. During the twentieth century, home-based jobs disappeared when new technologies spurred the creation of industries, large corporations, and big government. America became a nation of factory workers, office clerks, and civil servants.

New information technology enabled work to be done in the home once again. Still, many home businesses are not technology-related, although most do use a personal computer. Any way you cut it, the PC is the single biggest factor behind the home-business explosion.

Economic Insecurity

Economic insecurity is the second force driving the growth of home businesses. Despite the long-term economic boom in America, insecurity about what the future holds still plagues many people. Among those in the traditional world of work, global competition, mergers, downsizing, and bankruptcies are eroding the security that employment with a good company once offered. Concurrently, these economic developments are creating many new opportunities for home-based entrepreneurs (HBEs).

Many workers leave, or are laid off from, large companies and start home businesses to gain control over their work life. No job or career is secure because no company can effectively forecast its business situation beyond about 2 years. HBEs are able to spread their risk by working with different clients; losing a client who is experiencing a business downturn is easier to manage than losing a job. Others start businesses simply to cash in on new opportunities.

Many corporate managers now view human resources as "core" or "supplemental." Virtually every business has slack time and other periods when the demands on the company are greater. The challenge many managers face today is to structure their core staff—the people they need on a regular basis—to meet the core business demand. This prompts such managers to then think in terms of buying staff hours, both core, and supplemental. Former employees as home-based entrepreneurs often comprise the brunt of the supplemental staff.

A Conference Board study in the mid-1980s found that 12 million mid-level managers were systematically removed from the ranks of the corporate world either through lay-offs, dead-end careers, or other pressures. The trend continued throughout the 1990s. Most "displaced workers" opted for careers within existing small businesses or started their own ventures. More and more ex-corporate staff have the opportunity to work as independent consultants. Consultants tend to earn higher wages per hour, but they are almost always job-specific costs that can be negotiated and evaluated as each specific assignment is made.

Changes in Demographics

Tens of millions of the 74,000,000 baby boomers have reached the peak of their careers at the same time that corporate management jobs are being eliminated. By 2010, the typical large business will have cut its management ranks by two thirds or more. Facing limited opportunities for promotion, more employees in this age range will start their own businesses. One third or more of those will start from home.

Retired Americans are also starting home-based businesses in record numbers. The American Home-Based Business Association reports that a sizable percent of home-based businesses are run by retirees. As the average life span increases to 85 or 90 years, and eventually to 100, more seniors will work from home to supplement their pensions and social security.

Female-owned businesses continue to grow faster in number than male-owned ventures. The U. S. Small Business Administration says that women now own half of all businesses in America.

Restructured Families

The continuing dramatic changes in American family life also spur the growth of home-based business. Both married and single parents are setting up home offices to help juggle work and child care. Many have a pioneering attitude, inventing new rules for living and working as they go along.

Some work at home 1 or 2 days a week. One magazine editor works out of a converted sun room on the second floor of his home 2 days a week. Working at home lets him be around his two young children during the workday; it also allows him to get more "solo work" (such as writing and editing) finished than he could in the office.

THE BENEFITS OF MARKETING FROM HOME

If you're already operating a home-based business, you've discovered many benefits of marketing from home, which include but are not limited to:

- No warming up the car; no time lost commuting; no commuting stress; no auto accidents; longer car life; and reduced gasoline expense
- No additional rent or lease expense
- Moderate expenses for additional phone lines; moderate increases in expenses for utilities

- Enhanced ability to make and receive after-hours marketing calls; use of other equipment at will; more flexible hours
- Reduced wardrobe expense
- Enhanced ability to relax, rest, or nap at will; to eat more nutritious, well-balanced meals
- No need for extra keys, security cards, parking passes, lock combinations, and so forth

Marketing from your home office, particularly if you hold another job outside the home, helps to define and separate your two jobs. Lengthened work days become possible, with less fatigue, because you control many of the environmental factors.

The disadvantages, in many cases, stem from not having the discipline to capitalize on the advantages. For example:

- Making and answering phone calls at odd hours may become the norm rather than an exception.
- Napping, snacking, and home distractions may cut into vital marketing time. The opportunity to snack whenever you choose often leads to increased belt size.
- The stress and tension of working at an outside office may be replaced by a new kind of stress, i.e., attempting to do too much, being unfocused, or, ironically, becoming too successful as a home-based marketer.

Operating and marketing from a home office can disrupt home life, and small children can distract a parent from his or her business activities. What's more, the typical home office is often crammed into less space than the same entrepreneur might occupy in a commercial building or elsewhere outside the home.

WHAT KIND OF BUSINESSES CAN BE MARKETED FROM HOME?

What kinds of businesses are being started and marketed out of the home? Consultants account for more than one out of five home-based businesses. Other popular businesses include word-process-ing, mail order, accounting, real estate, and graphic arts businesses.

There are also home-based workers in interior decorating, insur-ance, advertising, communications and public relations, home remodeling, day care centers, bread-and-breakfast inns, weight and fitness counseling, tax and financial counseling, software develop-ment, recording, investment banking, executive recruiting, and sales.

IRS composite tax records reveal that light manufacturing and equipment repair, as well as ventures into tailoring, tutoring, and musical instruction, are all flourishing as home-based businesses. Add to these computer programming, desk-top publishing, tele-marketing, and telephone answering services. The list of businesses that can proficiently be operated or managed from the home is growing; following is a sample:

Actuary	Dietitian
Aerial photographer	Directory publisher
Antiques dealer	Disc-jockey service
Appraiser	Draftsperson
Architectural designer	E-mail software developer
Association founder	Electronic marketer
Audio engineer	Employment agency
Auctioneer	Engraver
Broadcast engineer	Errand service
Career counselor	Event clearinghouse
Carpet specialist	Event planner
Catalog publisher	Excavating service
Chiropractor	Exercise instructor
Cleaning service	Executive recruiter
Clown service	Expert-search firm
Comedian	Feed exporter
Computer animator	Fund raiser
Computer missionary	Geologist
Conference planner	Glass blower
Corporate communications	Gourmet caterer
Courseware developer	Graphic designer
Court reporter	Hair stylist
Design consultant	Hot-air balloon instructor

Housing consultant
Household-cleaner
Household repair
Hydroplane manufacturer
Indexer
Information broker
Insurance broker
Interior designer
Investment manager
Inventor
Jeweler
Landscaper
Laser-cartridge manufacturer
Legal software developer
Library management
Limousine service
Locksmith
Lyricist
Mailing-list services
Manufacturer's rep
Market research
Marketing agent
Massage therapist
Mechanic
Messenger service
Mobile-phone leasing
Mobile notary
Model-kit maker
Music engineer
Musician's network
Networking firm
Newsletter publisher
Nursing service
Office-automation
    consultant
Organic farmer
Organizer
Parking-lot maintenance

Party planner
Pest control
Pet care
Photo-newsletter publisher
Photography studio
Psychological services
Private investigator
Professional services
Publisher
Radio/TV voice-overs
Real estate appraiser
Relocation consultant
Researcher
Reunion planner
Remodeler
Roof inspector
Sales trainer
Script writer
Security consultant
Security and monitoring
Sign maker
Silk flower arranger
Shopping service
Speaker
Speech writer
Stockbroker
Strategist
Surveyor
Teaching nurse
Technical writer
Telecommunications analyst
Title abstracter
Tour operator
Transcriptionist
Translator
Travel agent
Urban planner
Vending machine operator

Wardrobe designer	Water purifier
Washing service	Woodworker
Waste consultant	

In short, if a business today can be run and marketed from a home-based setting, IT WILL BE! The stigma against professionals working out of the home has decreased to all-time lows as lawyers, accountants, architects, chiropractors, day-care providers, engineers, graphic artists, massage therapists, and psychologists open their front doors to greet clients.

What Kind of Person Starts a Home-Based Business?

Not everyone can start as fast as billionaire Michael Dell, who launched the fast-growing Dell Computer company from his college dorm room. The entrepreneurial drive, however, is alive and well for millions of Americans starting out at home.

There are two basic varieties of home-based entrepreneurs: those who started at home (either because they wanted to or had to) and those who moved an existing venture to home. Here are some brief profiles of entrepreneurs in different fields who started at home and have no intention of working anywhere else:

Book Publishers

Neighbors Arlene Simons and Peg Drummond each quit their jobs after having a first child. Soon both missed the challenge and fulfillment of working, as well as the income. Both had a wide variety of work experience and decided to start a home-based word-processing business.

Initially, they offered only word-processing services, later adding list management, repetitive letters, and a resume service. Now, the pair have become book publishers as well. They wrote and self-published a book on starting a home business. They sell the book through direct mail, by advertising in home-business newsletters, through online newsgroups, and at local trade fairs and exhibitions.

Their next project is publishing a children's newsletter with games, songs, and stories, which will be marketed through children's bookstores. They are also seeking to create an online version of the newsletter.

Custom Home Builder

Don Haynes is following the family tradition by working in the construction business. While his father is a commercial real estate developer, Don took the route of custom home building.

Don typically works on one job at a time. He hires afresh for every job. He has been using the same architecture firm for the past 3 years, but has run through an assortment of carpenters, bricklayers, plumbers, roofers, electricians, and painters.

He works out of a converted carriage house and maintains his office upstairs. He uses project management software to plan jobs and schedule workers. When he runs into difficulties, he plugs them into his schedule and can immediately see what adjustments he has to make.

Don also uses the computer to market his services. He keeps a referral list on disk and mails a newsletter twice a year to prospects who have inquired about his company. Don has no plans to move out of his home office. He has acquired off-site, locked storage space to keep blueprints and details of finished projects. Having a home office also helps Don weather the cyclical fortunes of the custom home market.

Strategic Planning Consultant

Lyza Benston knew she wanted to be on her own as a consultant helping companies chart their course. To prepare herself, she worked at a variety of positions: researcher with a consulting firm, corporate strategic planner, and director of the planning office for a state government. With all of that experience and a reputation in her field, Lyza hung out her shingle as Benston and Associates.

Lyza works with a variety of clients in the United States and is expanding her business overseas. Her business could not work without her computer and modem. Lyza teaches a course electronically at a university in California, even though she is based in Philadelphia, Pennsylvania. She uploads her lecture weekly, and her students download it. They post messages on the course bulletin board, to which Lisa and the other students respond for an electronic version of the classroom discussion.

Lyza's current clients include a school system in the Southwest trying to get social services in the schools to help better serve its poverty-stricken students, a telecommunications association seeking to market advanced phone features to minority customers, and a medium-sized paper company seeking to set up a system to better monitor changes in their business environment (which could have an effect on the firm's existing products).

Lyza finds working at home more relaxing than having a traditional office. Since most of her work is either writing (easily done at home) or consulting with clients out of the office, she feels she has no need for an elaborate home office.

If there is a pattern to successful home-based marketing, it likely entails many of the following characteristics. Successful entrepreneurs:

- Are persistent
- Base their decisions on factual information as often as possible
- Minimize their risks by venturing forward in small steps
- Learn by doing, actually read manuals, hire young computer experts to show them PC and Internet technology, and keep an open mind when it comes to embracing new ways of doing things
- Make a continual, total commitment to the needs of the business
- Make service their primary goal, even if they are not in a service business *per se*
- Initiate the business with minimum capital, which forces them to solve problems with wit and innovation
- Recognize the potential for having some fun in business
- Quickly identify their immediate supporting environment: suppliers, customers, employers, friends, relatives, and so on

A BUILT-IN OPPORTUNITY: MARKETING TO OTHER HOME-BASED BUSINESSES

The median household income of the work-at-home set (including those not self-employed) is greater than $50,000 per year. The home-based entrepreneur has become a desirable target for both large corporations and other home-business entrepreneurs. Far from being "loners" or "mavericks", terms applied in the early 1970s to those who sought to work on their own, more than three quarters of home-based entrepreneurs are married, and nearly an equal number have children.

The distribution of home-based workers by age is about the same for men and women. A slightly greater percentage of men work at home above age 55 than do women, reflecting the tendency of men to start post-retirement work activities. A somewhat greater share of women work at home between the ages of 25 and 34, reflecting the interest women of this age have in balancing work with care for young children.

If home-based workers need help, they often turn to other home-based entrepreneurs for marketing advice, word-processing services, help with research, or other services. Marketing from home-based business to home-based business is flourishing. Home-based entrepreneurs understand and readily respond to one another. They communicate faster, more freely, and with less formality than traditional business-to-business or business-to-home-based-business communication.

While I won't limit my focus in this book to marketing just to other home-based businesses, the salient point is that a large and ever-growing number of home-based entrepreneurs live within three to four blocks of your home and within your community. These entrepreneurs are your potential customers if they are aware of your products and services.

What products could be marketed to home businesses on the basis of occupation? Here are a few ideas:

- Accounting software with custom templates that accommodate the record-keeping needs of a veterinarian, or a writer, or a word processor.
- "Quick-start" guides that provide short tutorials on starting a home-based business, covering business planning, selecting equipment, etc., focusing on a particular type of business.
- "Business-to-business" coupon mailers to help home-based entrepreneurs market to each other.
- A membership association of home-based manufacturer's reps, or commercial artists, or financial planners.

Finding Other Home-Based Entrepreneurs

Given the market potential of calling on other home-based entrepreneurs within your local area, how can you quickly and easily identify appropriate targets?

- Look in the white pages of many metropolitan telephone books. The latter half of the book is devoted to business and professional listings. These listings often contain smaller, entrepreneurial enterprises, including a bevy of home-based entrepreneurs. Many of those listed within these white pages do not maintain listings in the Yellow Pages.
- Examine the listing. Home-based businesses that do advertise in the traditional Yellow Pages often can be detected from their addresses. For example, is the street address one that you know to be residential as opposed to commercial? Many single line entries, as opposed to quarter- and half-page advertisers, tend to be of the home-business variety.
- Find alternative directories. Mini-Yellow Pages serve the suburban areas of many major metropolitan areas. For example, in Falls Church, Virginia, outside of Washington, D.C., a half-inch-thick mini-Yellow Pages directory serves Falls Church, another serves Arlington, and another Alexandria. Each of these mini-directories contains only a

fraction of the number of businesses listed in the Northern Virginia Yellow Pages. Using the minis will enable you to spot other home-based businesses more quickly.

- Call the Chamber of Commerce in your town. It may maintain a roster of businesses or members and, once again, from the addresses you can detect who is operating from a residence.
- Search online for national small business associations such as the American Home-based Business Association and the National Association of Home-based Businesses. Many groups offer directories of their members.
- Check the business-card bulletin boards at your local printers and office supply stores. Many firms that display their business cards on such bulletin boards are home businesses.

A HOME MARKETER'S LAUNCH PLAN

Are you just starting your business? Added to the tips above on identifying other home-based marketers, here is a 5-month grand opening marketing plan, designed to help you gain clients or customers the moment you begin earning from home. Assuming you've decided on an April 1 official opening for a consulting business at your Caldwell home, here are action steps:

In December:

- Complete all directory listings in which you'll be included as soon as possible. This includes the Caldwell Yellow Pages (see Chapter 5) and mini-directories, plus other directories serving your local area.
- As soon as your new business name is established (see Chapter 3), prepare business cards and stationery. Include all applicable ways that customers or clients can reach you: fax numbers, beepers, e-mail addresses, and so on. Order a rubber stamp (or a set of pressurized labels to be used on business cards and stationery) announcing the actual date of the grand opening.

- Prepare a variety of public announcements and press releases (see Chapter 3) to be submitted 1 to 2 weeks before the opening, such as this one:

> *Joe Smith Consulting announces its opening at 825 Ashlawn Street in Caldwell on April 1, 2006. Joe Smith has 16 years of experience serving small businesses in the greater metro area. Appointments will be taken starting on the 15th of March.*

- Write press releases on your services, office facilities, and civic and professional activities.
- Visit the Caldwell Business Center or Chamber of Commerce and obtain information on seminars and club meetings to be held in the area in the coming 2 months. Similar information can be obtained by closely examining the business section of the *Caldwell Morning Times*. Attend as many Caldwell business functions as possible to make key connections. The fact that your new office is opening up in a convenient location is welcome news to many of the people you'll be meeting.
- Write to your college alumni newspaper with information about the new office. Several alumni live or work in the Caldwell area.

In January and February:
- Prepare invitations for your open house, to be distributed to all prospects in a three-block radius, as well as nearby office buildings. Hire a college student (see Chapter 11) to distribute these cards throughout the Caldwell area.
- Call then visit, the managers of the office supply stores nearby and ask if there's any promotional tie-in or reciprocal referral arrangement that you might undertake. The

tie-in, of course, has to be something you fully believe is beneficial to all concerned.

- Call all of the area condominium and high-rise building managers and ask for a copy of each building's newsletter. (A building manager may refer you to a publication's editor.) State that you're contemplating advertising in the newsletter; its staff will be more than happy to supply you with samples and helpful suggestions.

In March:

- Issue press releases to the local papers 5 to 7 days before the actual opening (see Chapter 3).
- Spruce up your home in every way (see Chapter 10). Clean the rug, repaint, replace fixtures, buy two more chairs. Visit other home-based entrepreneurs who receive clients or customers to gain ideas.
- Fifteen to 20 days before opening, have phones installed (if not already in place) so that appointments can be scheduled. With announcements indicating that appointments will be scheduled, it's important that a voice be at the other end of the phone number listed.

In April:

- Hold an open house. Start at 5 p.m. Pad the guest list with friends scheduled to arrive earlier than others so the event is well attended from the start. Rent extra chairs. Be ready to greet early guests who were not part of the early scheduled arrivals. A modest but well selected offering of wine and hors d'oeuvres will do nicely. Feel free to talk business.
- Collect business cards in a bowl.
- During the month, prepare announcement cards urging people to tell their friends about the new office. Then, as correspondents increase, double the value of all mail you send by including the Tell Your Friends card.
- Post a message on every community bulletin board in the area. If applicable, post the message on local Usenet bulletin boards.

Optional Activities Concurrent with Start-Up:
- Seek reciprocal promotional courtesies. This involves individually visiting nearby businesses and discussing how you and the proprietor may help each other's business.
- When patronizing other business establishments in Caldwell, such as restaurants or banks, take some of your office announcement cards and leave them in strategic locations; for example, near the teller's window at the bank or on the counter at the dry cleaner's.

HOT TIPS/INSIGHTS FROM CHAPTER 1

- Among others, these four factors have fueled the growth of home-based businesses: an explosion in information technology, economic insecurity, changing demographics, and restructured families.
- Many home businesses are not technology-related, although most do use a personal computer. The widespread use of the PC, however, remains the single biggest factor behind the home-business explosion.
- The acceptance of home-based businesses is, increasingly, not an issue. You can market out of your home with confidence.
- Home-based entrepreneurs tend to be an affluent market.
- Consultants account for more than one out of five home-based businesses. Other popular businesses include word processing, mail order, accounting, real estate, and graphic arts businesses.
- There are enough identifiable home-based entrepreneurs within your neighborhood or immediate community to constitute a lucrative market.
- Initiate grand opening plans well in advance of the date. You want as many clients or customers as possible from the start.

CHAPTER 2

What to Offer and from Where:
Your Marketing Command Center

Since the universe apparently is infinitely long in all directions, your home-based business office is in the center of the universe.

Regardless of whether you live in a detached single-family home, a high-rise condominium, a garden apartment, or any other structure, the office layouts that you can devise to support your marketing efforts vary widely. How you *feel* about marketing from your home office actually is more important than *where* it is located within your home. Your office needs to be comfortable and accessible for you. It has to be designed to support you, and if you choose to greet clients or customers at home (see Chapter 10), to influence them favorably.

In this chapter, I'll walk you through several settings, noting those factors that will give you the edge in marketing your business. (If you're ecstatic with your office as is, skim this chapter for ideas, and go on to the next.) First, however, we need to focus on positioning.

How Do You Want to Position Your Business?

The concept of positioning was popularized two decades ago by Al Ries and Jack Trout. They observed that, "In our over-communicated society, very little communication actually takes place." Rather, a company, even a home-based business, needs to create a position in the prospect's mind. Markets today are even less receptive to traditional marketing strategies. Too many products, too many companies, too many messages, and too many distractions command the attention of the customer; most marketing information is forgotten.

Think of positioning as an organized system for finding a window in the mind, recognizing that the most effective communication occurs when optimally placed and timed. Being the "first" remains one of the quickest and easiest ways to gain a position in someone's mind. Who was the first American woman in space? Without hesitation you can probably offer the name "Sally Ride." You are correct. Now name the second woman in space. If you are like most people, you will probably have no idea. (The answer is Judy Resnik, who was a member of the unfortunate Challenger Shuttle crew.)

Sometimes in thinking of how you want to position your business, you find yourself considering alternative uses for what you offer. Such thinking can lead to new opportunities in reaching your target market or perhaps to the ability to reach a new target market, and this may radically alter the type of office set-up that you employ.

Petroleum jelly was first promoted as a gel to heal burns or damaged skin. Later it was touted as a skin conditioner. In the past couple of years, television commercials have extolled its virtues as a make-up remover. Similarly, baking soda has gone through numerous repositioning evolutions. At various times it has been promoted as dentifrice, carpet cleaner, aid for your cat's box, and refrigerator deodorant.

When evaluating your products (and services for that matter) consider the opportunities if the following can be offered. Can your product or service be:

- Combined with something else?
- Made to do different jobs?
- Packaged more attractively?
- Produced at a lighter weight?
- Easier to clean?
- Enlarged?
- Reused?
- Less expensive?
- Faster?
- Portable?

For service firms, there are also many ways to reposition the services you provide. For example, temporary service firms traditionally placed secretaries and receptionists. However, many firms now place accountants, graphic artists, editors, and even managers.

Promoting a new use for your services enables you to build on your existing base and try new marketing approaches on limited capital. If the strategy doesn't work, you haven't lost much. Here are some suggestions for reassessing your service offering:

- Can you provide printed instructions?
- Will customer follow-up increase perceived value?
- Can you cut costs or materials and still provide the same service?
- Could you perform some aspect of the service at the customer's site?
- Could it be done in less time?
- Could you offer peripherals or accessories?
- Would renaming it increase its value?

Any shifts in what you offer to a greater or lesser degree will impact how you set up your marketing command center. In the larger sense, positioning is directly linked to how you set up your office, convey your image on paper and online (Chapters 3 and 4), and, of course, how you greet customers or clients at your home-based office (Chapter 10). I'll revisit the concept in the aforementioned chapters. For now, keep in mind that what you intend to offer, along with where in your home you choose to set up your office, can impact your marketing effectiveness.

A software instruction writer in Atlanta started receiving offers to train executives on using various software applications. Suddenly, his single desk and single PC were inadequate. He rearranged his office so that a 3- by 18-shelf- bin-type unit could be installed behind him.

Thereafter, he could simply use a swivel chair to turn and face the bins to pick and choose the paper stock he would use for his workbook to be distributed to his students.

He also rearranged his office to accommodate a flipchart, large wall calendar, and floor plants. He figured that the more comfortable, decorative, and well-equipped his office, the more productive and creative he would be—and he was right.

Several weeks later, he installed a sophisticated voicemail system, changed his ventilation and lighting, and refurnished his bathroom. While client/visitors were rare, he ran his office as if one might call on him at any time.

Your Office and Your Positioning

If you'll be receiving visitors, your task is clear—upgrade your office to that of a highly successful entrepreneur in your field. Even if you never encounter visitors/clients, your position is developed by the phone and answering systems you employ and your phone greeting and manner. Your stationery, logo, and printed literature, as well as your website, also play a large part (all covered in subsequent chapters). The key questions to ask yourself when setting up a home office are: does it support your marketing, does it meet the expectations of your target market, and does it further enhance the position I wish to retain in the minds of those I hope to serve?

Let's turn now to common office arrangements.

The Den Office

The den office (and here a spare bedroom counts as a den) is the most popular among home-based marketers and provides the greatest number of advantages. If you have a den or spare-bedroom office or a detached office, you are apt to enjoy more benefits than with an office in another part of your home, such as the attic or basement, or on the dining-room table. Heating, cooling, and ventilation are apt to be more easily controlled from the den office.

Proximity to the front door is useful when greeting visitors and for making your own quick exits. The advantage of proximity to the bathroom is obvious.

All Quiet on the Business Front

Even in a custom-designed home-based office, you need to control communications with the outside world. Between the telephone, fax, and e-mail, the potential exists for an environment with as many interruptions as you would experience in a commercial office.

If you live alone, any portion of your home that you carve out for home-office purposes can ably serve to support your marketing efforts.

A den or spare-bedroom office in a home with a spouse or children (or roommates), may not give you the privacy and quiet that you need to do your best work. If this is the case, many options exist to soundproof and cordon off your office space. Room dividers and sound barriers are available in a wide variety of shapes and sizes; placed in front of your desk or outside the door to your office, they can improve any existing sound barriers.

One work-at-home graphic artist turns on a small fan next to her office door. The gentle, rhythmic white noise of the fan's motor serves as a sound buffer, absorbing most of the sounds her husband makes in the rest of the apartment. Some home-based marketers prefer soft classical music or harmless Muzak-type backgrounds to serve as a buffer to other distracting sounds. Various white-noise and sound-dampening gadgets are available today through direct mail catalogs and at popular electronics stores. They mask out the sounds behind them (such as noisy kids) and quickly pay for themselves.

Other than when a client is visiting you on site, the telephone represents your key mode of verbal conversation. Therefore, you need to feel comfortable and well supported in using the telephone (see Chapter 6). You'll know you have achieved the right balance when you are able to make or receive a phone call at any time and have no fear of distraction or disruption.

Here is a listing of the advantages and disadvantages of the den-type office:

Advantages
- Proximity to the rest of the house
- Heating, cooling, and ventilation control
- Proximity to bathroom
- Proximity to front entrance
- Ease of receiving/meeting clients

Disadvantages
- May not offer desired level of privacy
- May not be soundproof
- May be too small, or lack sufficient storage space
- May lack desired electrical outlets
- May foster undesired positioning

The Detached or Semi-Detached Office

The detached or semi-detached office is mandatory if you are a lawyer, doctor, or dentist. A semi-detached office is a completely finished room or set of rooms adjacent to or part of your home's overall structure that is otherwise not a part of your home. Ideally you would have both an entrance for clients and a passageway to the rest of your home.

The detached office offers privacy, can be decorated and furnished in complete contrast to your home, and provides most of the marketing advantages of a commercial office. Because many people are familiar with and have been comfortable over the years visiting a dentist who operates from a detached office, it is a structure that readily gains the approval of those doing business with you for the first time. (Chapter 10, "To Greet and Meet," elaborates on how to create a visitor-friendly office or meeting area.)

If you have a reception or waiting room, you can furnish it to enhance your overall marketing effort. If you leave magazines or other literature in the outer office for visitors to read, forget *People*, *Time*, and *Newsweek*. Instead display upscale periodicals such as *Atlantic*, *Forbes*, *Fortune*, *Harpers*, *Executive Female*, or even *Business Week*. Also provide one or two key publications specific to your industry.

If you are an attorney, for example, you could display the *ABA Journal*, *Barrister*, *Legal Economics*, or *Practical Lawyer*. If you are an advertising or communications consultant, you can display *Advertising Age*, *Advertising Week*, *Public Relations Journal*, or *Marketing News*.

These publications subtly convey to visitors that you are professionally minded. While visitors are unlikely to suspect that a professional who doesn't display such publications is less than professionally minded, providing them indicates that you have the right touch. The client or customer is more likely to feel he/she made a good decision in coming to your office.

Especially for professionals who are reticent to ask existing clients for referrals, proper decor in the waiting room is just what the doctor ordered. As I discussed in *Marketing Your Consulting and Professional Services* (Wiley, 1997), one of my clients, a dentist, was shy when it came to asking patients to recommend potential new patients. We solved the problem by putting up an attractive sign with eye-catching print in his waiting room that read:

> *New Patient Referrals*
>
> *Cheerfully Accepted*

In any case, make sure that your waiting room encourages clients and visitors who can send new business your way.

- Keep several dozen business cards readily available for the taking in a cardholder.
- If you have brochures, pamphlets, capability statements, article reprints, and the like, display multiple copies of these on the coffee or end table or even in a literature rack that invites a visitor to take them.
- Display plaques, certificates, licenses, and awards.
- If you provide samples, display them.
- If you provide a service, leave an elegant notebook with letters from satisfied customers enclosed in clear plastic sheet protectors.

Here is a listing of the advantages and disadvantages of the detached or semi-detached office:

Advantages
- Connotes professionalism to visitors
- Can be decorated and furnished altogether differently from the rest of your home
- Generally more spacious
- Waiting room can encourage visitors to make referrals
- Ease of employing staff, e.g., receptionists, part-timers
- Ease of leaving the office physically and mentally at the end of the workday

Disadvantages
- Separate and higher rate phone bill
- Separate and higher rate utility bill
- May require commercial cleaning service
- May be subject to more solicitations

The Attic Office

Karl refinished his attic so that he could set up his home office there. Except for excessive heat in the summer, which he was able to control with a room air conditioner and a set of fans, the attic office was more than adequate. It offered ample space. He set up tables to handle various projects in progress and installed a cot so that he could take quick catnaps during the day without coming downstairs.

Karl quickly found that the distance to the kitchen and the bathroom was a problem. Every time he wanted a drink of water, he had to make a trip downstairs. He started bringing a pitcher of water upstairs and soon installed a small refrigerator. However, each time he went to the bathroom and each time he forgot something from downstairs, a trip down the stairs was necessary.

Depending on the specifics of your location, there are some distinct advantages to maintaining an attic office:

Advantages
- If space is sufficient, you will be able to lay out several projects at once.

- You can set up substations for specific tasks, which is particularly helpful when using part-time employees.
- It may offer excellent privacy and desirable isolation.
- Your view from on high may foster creative thinking.

Disadvantages
- You tend to hear and be aware of all changes that take place under you (i.e., someone coming in the front door).
- Lack of proximity to the entrance and other aforementioned stops can be annoying.
- The office may not be suitable for meeting clients.
- Rain, branches striking your roof, and a whole new cast of disturbances may arise.
- Heating and air conditioning may pose special problems.

The Basement Office

Alexis is a small-business broker, helping clients to buy or sell businesses. She lives in a seven-room, three-story townhouse in Wilmette, Illinois, north of Chicago. The basement includes her office, a storage room, and the laundry room. Because the door to the basement is directly adjacent to the front door, Alexis is easily able to meet clients in her basement office.

She has two additional phone lines (for fax and Internet), an answering service, and an answering machine, so she is covered around the clock. Wall-to-wall shag carpeting and moderately priced furniture keep the room comfortable, but not overdone.

Alexis has one chair for visitors by the side of her desk, a four-seat circular table to the far left of her desk, a couch with a parallel coffee table, and some other chairs on the opposite side of the room. With this variety of furniture groupings, Alexis is able to meet up to four people at a time comfortably.

To keep her office visitor-friendly, Alexis stocks it with pads and pens, two hand-held calculators, and a phone extension a mere 20 feet from her desk phone. Alexis wants her clients to feel at ease at her home office and see it as a meeting place highly conducive to doing business. Last fall she installed a finished half-bathroom, and next year she will be installing wood paneling.

Rick provides management assistance to professional service organizations. He also maintains a basement office or, more accurately, offices. As one proceeds downstairs from the upstairs hallway, to the right is a finished den with bookcases, a television set, and a couch.

To the left is a hallway that leads past the laundry room, then another small room that Rick uses for storage, supplies, and files, and then his main office. He keeps on hand only those few items that he is currently working on and houses large filing cabinets, a storage locker, portable files, and two shelving units in the secondary office.

Although there is an outside entrance to the hallway leading to Rick's office, he practically never uses it. Instead, he leads the few clients who do visit through the living room to the dining room table where appropriate materials, dictation equipment, pads, and pens are kept.

Jean represents a third type of home-based marketer operating from a basement office. She is located in Annapolis, Maryland, and provides EDP (electronic data processing) seminars and instruction to area firms, the Naval Academy, and other agencies of the federal government.

Jean uses her expansive basement to house her computer, printer, and several flip charts and drawing boards. She uses an intercom that is always left in the "on" position to monitor the activities of her son who stays in a sectioned-off playroom, also within the basement. On days when Jean works on-site at a client's location, the child and his nanny remain on the main floor of the house for meals, playtime, and bathing.

The advantages of maintaining a basement office in terms of supporting your marketing efforts include:

Advantages
- If space is sufficient, you will have the ability to lay out several projects at once.
- You can set up substations for specific tasks, which is particularly helpful if you will be using part-time employees.
- A basement office can offer the right amount of privacy and isolation.

Disadvantages
- Basements tend to be cold (cold air falls).
- You tend to hear and be aware of all changes that take place above you (i.e., someone coming in the front door).
- Lack of proximity to the entrance way, bathroom, and other areas can be an irritant.
- The office may not be suitable for meeting clients.

The Dining-Room Table Office

The dining-room table, another table, or a corner of your home can effectively support you in your home-business marketing efforts under the following conditions:

- You are sales representative for a company with headquarters elsewhere.
- You are a part-time entrepreneur, or the revenue you derive from your home-office venture is not crucial to your income.
- Your venture doesn't require a lot of paperwork, notes, files, materials, etc.
- You have a few key accounts, and the work that you do for them can be performed in a small area (e.g., you proofread for a monthly magazine).
- You derive most or all of your income via online connections.
- You are an extremely organized person and have supporting resources.
- You live alone or have an extremely understanding spouse.

Sheila is a sales representative for a photography studio. Through an agreement with a national diaper service, the studio offers free baby pictures to new parents. Sheila's job is to deliver the free picture, already taken, and to attempt to sell reprints of the other proofs shot during the photo session.

Using a list prepared for her, Sheila's marketing task is to call the parents (usually the mother) and schedule an appointment. She also makes follow-up calls when a couple is thinking about ordering. All of her business is conducted outside the home; other than writing up orders, Sheila does not need to keep any elaborate records.

Sheila regards herself as self-employed, although that is not the true nature of her job. For her marketing activities, the dining-room-table office with a phone and a calculator is perfectly adequate.

Barbara is a sales representative for a nationally known insurance company. Barbara has a full-time receptionist/secretary and a well equipped office in town. At home, Barbara maintains a dining-room-table office, though her dining-room table is actually clear. She uses stacking plastic trays to maintain a healthy volume of files and work-related papers on the credenza to the right of the table.

Like Sheila, Barbara never greets clients at home, so the appearance of her home-office substation is not important. Barbara has compromised the ambience and appearance of her dining room, but that doesn't bother her. She also keeps files in her upstairs bedroom in and on top of a two-drawer filing cabinet. This combination of outposts is sometimes more disruptive than helpful.

Barbara often spends considerable time searching through her files, frequently overcopies, and has visibly growing clutter in all three locations. Are you a little like Barbara?

Here is a quick summary of the marketing advantages of the dining-room-table home office:

Advantages
- A reasonable option if no other space is available
- Work materials can quickly be assembled and disassembled as needed
- Usually provides sufficient table space to spread out work-related materials
- Lighting is usually excellent
- Provides a chance to be near other members of the family, if that is an objective
- Assembling and disassembling work materials, if handled correctly, can actually promote orderliness and efficiency
- Close to all household amenities

Disadvantages
- Quickly and frequently leads to clutter
- Generally is not conducive to sustained growth or expansion
- Can be disruptive to home life
- Subject to distractions and lack of privacy
- Files and paperwork can be lost or stained

Renters Beware

If you rent your current residence, then the nature of your lease can have implications for the effective marketing of your business. If you are planning to stay in the same location for a specific number of years, is your lease structured so that you can automatically renew as it expires? If not, you may find that you have sunk considerable funds into advertising and marketing literature that soon may contain an outdated address and phone number. While gummed labels denoting address or phone-number changes can alleviate some short-term problems, having to relocate your office is disruptive in more costly ways.

The time to consider how your lease may impact your business is before disruption can cause any harm. Here are some questions to consider sooner rather than later:

- Is your landlord willing to consider an immediate extension of your present lease?
- Is your landlord willing to consider automatic, year-long or multi-year extensions?
- What happens if the property is sold or changes hands?
- Can you remodel or make modifications? If so, who pays for such improvements?

Your landlord will be more inclined to cover the renovation expense if the work you seek to have done will benefit future tenants after you leave.

Is Your Office Supporting You?

Regardless of where in the home you locate your office, there is one key question to determine whether you can be an effective marketer from there: *Does your office support you?*

If you have the space to assemble the equipment and supplies you need, and can arrange them so you can work in a highly effective and productive way, you're well on your way!

HOT TIPS/INSIGHTS FROM CHAPTER 2

- The office layouts you can devise to support your marketing efforts vary widely. How you *feel* about marketing from your home office is more important than *where* it is located.
- It's hard to market effectively from home if you do not find your office to be comfortable.
- A detached or semi-detached office offers the greatest marketing advantages.
- Professional publications in your entrance way or reception area subtly convey to visitors that you are professionally minded.
- Make sure that your waiting room encourages clients and visitors who can send new business your way; keep several dozen business cards and literature readily available.
- Basement offices tend to offer the most space and hence the ability to lay out several projects at once.
- You know you've created an effective home office when you are able to make or receive a phone call at any time and have no fear of distraction or disruption.

CHAPTER 3

Your Image in Print

The first impression anyone has about your business often comes from what they read about you in hard copy or online. In that respect, you can look as good as you want to look.

This chapter is about your image in print: how your stationery, logo, brochure, and other printed materials, as well as Web site, e-mail signature and other online information, impacts prospects, people who have not yet met or spoken to you.

As we saw in Chapter 2, positioning is a way of thinking rather than a fixed set of guidelines or principles. The position that your business develops in your market or industry often may be right only for you and for no other business. You may become the leader in a local emerging niche, or a highly successful alternative company to the leading company in a mature market. You may be the only service available on weekends or the most exclusive firm exhibiting wares by appointment only. Position marketing is not limited to a particular strategy.

Positioning can be enhanced through advertising, public relations, your company's location, and even the way in which you are financed. Regardless of how it becomes established, the position you occupy in the minds of those you wish to serve contributes to the success or failure of the business. What you convey to your target market via your printed materials has as much to do with establishing your position as nearly anything else you do.

Realistically, your ability to market effectively from a home-based business often boils down to how you respond when asked, *Can you send me something?* Or, *Do you have a Web site?*

Let's start with traditional printed materials first and cover the nuances of being online in the next chapter. The first impression prospects have of you and your services or products may well be literature from you or about you. In a sense, your printed literature helps carve out your position in the minds of those you wish to reach. According to Ries and Trout, effective positioning, in the long run, can help to further your business's progress toward desired revenues, even in the face of limited capital!

The more complex society becomes, the more crucial it is for you to carve out a distinctive business territory. Each year, *Forbes* magazine profiles and analyzes 200 of the country's best small companies. The common denominator among these companies is their ability to develop a highly refined niche. As observed in *Forbes*, "Once there was ice cream. Now there is ice cream, superior premium ice cream, and elbowing in between them, premium ice cream. The ice cream afficionado knows the difference."

Successful companies define themselves (or redefine themselves) in very precise terms, and this shows up on their printed literature. When you've positioned yourself well, each piece of literature and message contributes to the delivery of a consistent theme to the target market. By securing a well placed corner in the minds of those you wish to serve, you can reduce the need for new costly marketing campaigns.

Here's a run-through of some of the common tools that you can use to enhance your image, establish a position, and thus support your overall marketing efforts.

STATIONERY

The most effective stationery, and exceptions abound, contains an attractive letterhead with a distinctive logo on fine paper stock that is off-white. You don't need to spend a small fortune to develop an attractive, eye-catching letterhead; the fastest and least expensive way is to begin a file of the letterheads and stationery that you receive from others—a technique I recommend for developing any printed materials. Then draw upon the best of the best.

Ask yourself about each item:

- Does the style of printing attract you?
- How big is the logo and where is it placed?
- What color is the paper? The printing?
- What is the weight, texture, and feel of the paper?

Samples of stationery are presented on the next few pages together with the advantages and disadvantages of their features.

The first, my own, is printed on a light blue fading to light green paper. Yes, there's a ton of fine print in the upper right-hand corner, but it saves me an awful lot of time recounting book titles. It also opens doors faster.

The letters CMC, following my name, stand for certified management consultant. They lend more credibility to me as a business professional. Here are some of the advantages and disadvantages of my letterhead:

Advantages
- The layout is unusual and eye-catching.
- A blank space of $\frac{1}{2}$" allows for more effective faxing.
- It can be updated at will.
- The letterhead can also serve as a cover page for other things.

Disadvantages
- Lacks the image punch a bigger firm could present
- May be "too much" for some people, or print may be too small

Professional speaker, certified management consultant, and author of 2700 articles and 25 books, among them:

Breathing Space: Living & Working at a Comfortable Pace in a Sped-up Society (MasterMedia)
Selling to the Giants: How to Be a Key Supplier to Large Corporations (McGraw-Hill)
Marketing Your Consulting & Professional Services, 3rd edition (John Wiley)
Blow Your Own Horn: How to Get Noticed and Get Ahead (Berkley)
The Complete Idiot's Guide to Managing Your Time (Macmillan)
Avoiding the Pitfalls of Starting Your Own Business (Lifetime)
The Complete Idiot's Guide to Managing Stress (Macmillan)

The Complete Idiot's Guide to Assertiveness (Macmillan)
Marketing for the Home-Based Business (Adams Media)
The Complete Idiot's Guide to Goal-setting (Macmillan)
Power And Protocol for Getting to the Top (Newbridge)
Marketing on a Shoestring, 2nd edition (John Wiley)
How to Have a Good Year Every Year (Berkley)
Getting New Clients, 2nd edition (John Wiley)

Jeff Davidson, MBA, CMC
BREATHING SPACE® INSTITUTE
2417 Honeysuckle Road, Suite 2A
Chapel Hill NC 27514-6819 USA
(919) 932-1996 ▪ (FAX) (919) 932-9982 ▪ Jeff@BreathingSpace.com   http://www.BreathingSpace.com

Catherine Fyock's letterhead is a slightly darker beige with solid black printing only. The shadowing effect of the letters IMC (Innovative Management Concepts) offers a three-dimensional effect so that the initials serve as a logo while drawing attention to Fyock's message: "Specialists in Finding, Choosing, Training, and Retaining Key Employees in a Labor Shortage Market."

The post office box number, town, state, zip code, and telephone number are readable, if slightly disharmonious with the logo, and perhaps are better placed at the bottom of the page. The box number signifies that this is a home-based business, which is something the entrepreneur may wish to signify since she has positioned herself as a specialized consultant.

Advantages

- Inexpensive to produce
- Photocopies well
- Conveys the image of a solo consultant
- Message under logo tightly defines services offered

Disadvantages
- Print runs too close to left and right border, may be truncated when photocopied
- Box number without street address makes some people feel uneasy
- Lack of second color may signal lower quality image

Dave Yoho's use of a sketch in the corner of his stationery and its landscape orientation have long positioned him as a distinctive speaker, management consultant, and sales trainer. Speaking to many groups across the United States each year, Dave uses a letterhead that conveys that he is a unique individual, someone who has enjoyed numerous achievements and considerable success over his long career.

While Dave is not a home-based entrepreneur, let's learn from the way he uses his letterhead. Because of the quality of the paper and the unique layout, his stationery stands out. With the addition of the standard contact information, Dave's message comes across, regardless of what any particular letter says.

Advantages
- Distinctive and memorable
- Consistent with Dave's personality and the type of service he provides
- Lends an aura of high-level business consulting and professionalism

Disadvantages
- Some targets may find it unappealing
- May be counterproductive for business purposes, i.e., when the correspondence is lengthy and continues to additional pages
- Sketch changes as he ages
- Can initially be expensive; requires finding the right artist
- May not photocopy or fax well on some equipment

Whatever you do in your business, look for opportunities to use the name of your building on your stationery and literature. For example, if you live at 123 Mount Hope Road in the River House Apartment building, place *The River House* on your business card

DAVE YOHO ASSOCIATES
10803 West Main Street, Fairfax, VA 22030 (703) 591-2490
FAX (703) 273-6626

CONSULTING — SPEECHES — VIDEO TRAINING

Recipient
The Cavett
National Speakers
Association's "Oscar"

Gold Record
R.C.A. Victor Recording

Author
"How To Have A Good
Year Every Year"
Berkley Publishing

and literature above the street address. This adds an aura that is not generated simply by using the ordinary street address.

LOGOS THAT ENHANCE MARKETING

A logo is a symbol or stylized lettering that captures the essence of who you are and what you offer. The best logos are simple but powerful. Recall the Texaco star, the handwritten look of the word Kellogg's on cereal boxes, the silhouette of a driving basketball player (actually it's the legendary Jerry West) on the NBA's logo, or the spinning globe of AT&T.

The logo, whether a symbol or stylized lettering, is (if properly used) a graphic theme that runs through your stationery, flyers, brochures, business cards, and other printed materials. If you don't have a logo or have one and want to change it, here are some quick tips for finding a logo that is right for you:

1. Start with your company's initials or your own. Can an extension of one letter be used to cover the other two or wrap around them? What about shadowing initials such as Catherine Fyock did with the letters IMC? Try an ascending or descending pattern. Look for ways to make the parts of one letter connect with part of the next letter, such as the way Aetna logo connects the A and E.

2. Visit your local printer or stationer to review the display album for ordering business cards. The typical album will hold several hundred cards and provide you with a wealth of ideas for your logo. Copy or quickly jot down any that catch your eye, and once back home consider variations that may result in your unique logo. You'll need spare paper and felt-tip pens of different colors.

3. Go online and visit some of the more innovative web sites. In as little as a 10-minute session you'll be able to gather at least a half-dozen ideas that potentially could be adapted to what you're seeking to convey.

4. Call the art department of your local high school or community college and hire an art student for a couple of hours.

For as little as $20, a creative student may be able to sketch out a variety of logos, one of which can ultimately be developed into your final selection.

5. Visit the library and ask to see several books and magazines on the graphic arts. As you flip through the pages many ideas for a logo may spring up.

6. Poll your friends, relatives, and clients as to what type of logo they think would best serve your purposes. You may be surprised at the insight and consistency of the responses.

7. Walk around your own office and home and notice the logos on products you already own, i.e., the Quaker on Quaker Oats, the distinctive printing of Radio Shack, or a Black and Decker kitchen product you may own.

BROCHURES

When Brochures Are Useful and Recommended

Here are the cases when it probably makes sense for you to produce a brochure:

- Prospective clients frequently call or write you and ask for a brochure.
- The type of service or product that you offer is best introduced by an extended explanation.
- You often find that people who are in need of your service or product didn't know it exists, have never heard of it, or require educational, technical, or descriptive information.
- The nature of your business is such that you cannot effectively speak with each prospect who calls.
- Differentiating your service or product from others is difficult.

The fastest way to assemble your brochure, as explained in *Marketing Your Consulting and Professional Services* (Wiley, 1997), is to assemble the brochures of others in your industry and choose the best from the best. Always keep a file of the literature of your competitors or, if you don't have direct competitors, near-competitors.

When a Brochure Is *Not* Necessary

Many home-based businesses do not require brochures, so before you spend a couple of thousand dollars on one, carefully determine if your business even needs one. Here are a variety of situations in which you may not need a brochure:

- You offer consulting services to a specific target niche in which you are already well established.
- You sell products or services to a constituency that primarily find your company via the Internet.
- You easily write effective management letters and thus can offer a convincing one-on-one correspondence instead of sending a brochure.
- You have had articles published and have made attractive, high-quality reprints on glossy stock.
- You generate most of your new clients from seminars and lectures that you offer, and your business cards or other seminar handouts effectively induce prospects to contact you.
- Your business is evolving, and you will be offering different services or products, possibly from a different location or to different targets.

When you feel it is time to develop your own brochure, lay out on your desk or dining-room table the ten best brochures of others in your industry. Note the size, type of paper, colors used, pictures used, and flaps, if any.

As you review others' brochures, depending on the type of product or service you offer, you may discover yet more ways to serve customers, and hence increase your overall marketing effectiveness, by offering to them one or more of the following:

- Product or service discounts
- Product or service time extensions

- Free estimates, samples, or analyses
- Exclusive or charter memberships
- Quality or group discounts
- Extended warranties
- Additional products or services for no extra cost
- Extended telephone consultant privileges
- Extended memberships, life memberships
- Reduce costs on peripheral items or services
- Finder fees for new customers

The brochure and mix offering you decide upon need not be elaborate. In terms of its physical appearance, 8½" × 11", lightweight stock, folded into thirds to form a 3²/₃" × 8½" face, is sufficient. This size fits neatly in a #10 envelope or can be sent directly through the mail without an envelope. Note: If your home is hard to find, include a simplified map on your stationery, brochures, and other marketing support literature.

A business flyer can be a viable alternative to a brochure. For many businesses a flyer, typeset or near-typeset (good desk-top quality) on your letterhead or letterhead-quality paper, is effective for promoting your services or products. In lieu of letterhead, non-garish, colored paper such as light blue, light green, or grey can also be used.

Using the Brochure to Highlight Your Home-Based Business

Many entrepreneurs accent the fact that they operate out of their homes. Trainer and author Brian Tracy appeared in a major feature story about highly successful home-based entrepreneurs. The story contained several color photos of his office and surroundings.

So don't be afraid to use indoor photos of your office or of yourself meeting with clients if such pictures help position you appropriately. As long as you convey the image of a high-quality home-based business, you can't go wrong.

To emphasize the personal, individualized touch that you can offer your clients or customers, here is promotional copy you can adapt for your brochure or other printed literature:

- "...a home-based business serving customers from the same location for X years."
- "...all of the advantages of dealing with a downtown business, without the high price."
- "...personalized attention that you can't get anywhere else, handling all clients on a one-to-one basis—the only way they want it."
- "...when it's too important to have it get lost in a large company."
- "...the no-frills way to accomplish your goals."

Here's a roster of key attributes you can use in your printed literature when both differentiating yourself from other businesses and offering prospects an added measure of assurance:

Reliability involves consistency of performance and dependability. It means that your firm performs the service right the first time and that you honor your promises. Specifically, it involves accuracy in billing, keeping records correctly, and performing the service at the designated time. If this is one of your strengths, let it be known!

Responsiveness relates to your willingness and readiness to provide service. Specifically it involves, for example, sending a transaction slip immediately, calling a client or prospect back quickly, and giving prompt service (e.g., setting up appointments as requested). This is one of the prime reasons why someone may choose to do business with you over a downtown firm.

Competence means possessing the required skills and knowledge to perform the services you purport to offer. Dig through your professional past to derive every shred of evidence that you can do the job with gusto.

Access means being approachable and easy to reach (i.e., your telephone line is not incessantly busy; callers are not subject to endless rounds of voice mail instructions), waiting time to receive service is minimal, and your location is convenient.

Courtesy involves politeness, respect, consideration, and friendliness of contact personnel (including receptionists, telephone operators, etc.). It also includes consideration for the client's property (e.g., no muddy shoes on the carpet); clean and neat

Words with Universal Appeal

Here are things people want: to acquire, to save, to experience.

Here are things people want to acquire: health, wealth, friends, praise, acceptance, time, beauty, a sense of accomplishment, self-confidence.

Here are things people want to save: work, effort, time, energy.

Here are things people want to experience: old age, relaxation, recreation, love, prestige.

appearance of public contact personnel. This is a bigger factor these days than you might first consider. Think about how you feel as a customer toward others who show you little courtesy versus great courtesy.

Credibility means conveying trustworthiness, believability, honesty, and having the client or prospect's best interests at heart. Many factors contribute to credibility, such as your company name and reputation, your personal characteristics, and the degree of hard sell involved (less is better) in interactions with the client or prospect.

PHOTOS ADD TO THE MIX

Great photos can help your positioning efforts. Kevin Trolley, a Chicago based entrepreneur, says "a vibrant photograph in a newspaper's business section, an important trade journal, or a major news magazine can say much about a company's own vibrancy to customers, employees and investors."

One freelance photographer notes that "the news media, and in particular the publications read by those who can influence a company's growth, need good photos."

What kind of photographs can you use? Reception area, products, customer letters, your customers, your customers' facilities, yourself, your office, you in action, or anything generally related to the industry of your customers, are among the many appropriate subjects for photos. You can use photos to convey the underlying theme of quality, value, and service.

To keep your personal image updated, go to the photographer approximately once per year and get eight or ten different shots taken. I continually use different pictures on book jackets, magazine articles and in press releases (discussed at length on page xxx) to gain added exposure and recognition. It is almost disturbing to see the same picture of someone used over and over for years.

You have several options when you hire a photographer to have your picture taken:

- The head and shoulder shot is one that you will be able to use for virtually all types of promotion.
- You may wish to have action photos taken as well. This type of photo might include you in front of a seminar group, receiving an award, or conferring with a colleague. Action photos can occasionally be staged in the photographer's studio, but more often have to be taken on the spot.
- The candid shot is another useful photo. In candid photos you are seated at your desk or in some other familiar home-type or working environment that gives the reader a sense of your surroundings. Some photographers are equipped to create this type of environment right within their studio. Obviously, it is best to check in advance.

PUBLICITY IN THE LOCAL PAPERS

Pick up your area's business magazines or even the business section of your daily newspaper. Every issue of these publications carries an interview with or feature on a local entrepreneur. The majority of these stories are *placed by public relations firms who have been paid by the person for whom the story is about*. The profiles you see are a part of a coordinated effort initiated and funded by the company or individual publicized; those being featured are paying for it.

Suppose you help restore historic buildings in the Kansas City area, and the city council has voted to restore a historic building. One well placed interview, featuring you, on the significance of this structure to the community is likely to catch the eye of hundreds of builders and developers, preservation groups, historical societies, and anyone else concerned with architecture and historic preservation.

A Cleveland-based sculptor wanted to increase his visibility in the community and attract new business. To highlight and promote his line of products, he announced that he would sponsor an urban sculpture award (participants would use only junk hardware parts.) He had "in progress" and "completion" photos taken. A public relations agent was hired from the outset to ensure maximum exposure. A few weeks after the awards were judged, a major story appeared in one of the region's most prestigious monthly magazines under the by-line of the publicity agent.

To the average reader, it appeared that the publication had either contracted with the writer to produce this story or took the piece "over the transom." Because publishers have long known of the healthy number of entrepreneurs in their community who wish to be written about and who have the funds to commission an article, publishers often get their material for free.

The manner in which the name of the sculptor is publicized does not appear as an advertisement but as an article of social or community interest. An article is far more influential than an ad taken out by that same company.

Why does publicity like this pay? For one thing, it's not necessarily more costly or difficult to get an article written and placed than simply to pay for an ad. The cost of getting an article written, which may span several pages and include photos, is likely to cost far less than a single page ad in the same publication. While the advance planning, coordination, and acceptance of the self-generated article requires considerable effort, it is often a sound investment.

The next time you see an item in print about a company or individual with whom you compete, take an extra moment and consider how it got there.

GENERATING FREE PUBLICITY

Can you emulate the same effects that a high-priced publicist can achieve? Sometimes. Many otherwise effective home-based marketers of services miss out on opportunities to gain additional free publicity. These entrepreneurs don't realize that what they do professionally is news, at least to the town news, community features, and names in the news editors of local newspapers.

Remember: the people who get coverage usually initiate the process themselves. Any one of a number of events that will occur in the coming year in the life of your business may serve as material for a press (news) release:

- Will you be winning an award?
- Are you going to be speaking to a group in town?
- Will you be attending a convention?
- Is anything out of the ordinary about to occur?

These events and a host of others qualify as fodder for good press releases.

Good Topics for News Releases about Your Home-Based Business

Your Business Activities
- Anniversary of your company
- Citations, honors and awards
- Articles published
- Speeches given
- Launching a Web site
- Conferences attended
- Elections to club or association office
- Television or radio talk show guest
- Unique or outstanding accomplishments
- Joint ventures
- Long-term projects
- Relocation from commercial office to home office

Your Services or Products
- Research you have completed
- New service or new product offering

- Elaborate or unusual equipment you have purchased
- Initiation of new projects
- Free information or literature you have available

Your Business
- Club memberships
- Intern programs
- Participation with local institution
- Unique accomplishments
- Monthly, quarterly, or annual forecast
- Awards you give to others
- Surveys you have conducted

Survey on the Spot I lectured to the National Capital Speakers Association on the topic of using articles to help market one's speaking capabilities. The night I was speaking there were fifty members and guests in attendance. As part of my presentation, I invited the group to share with me how I was going to generate publishable survey information right in front of their eyes.

I asked them how many wanted to get published, and all fifty hands went up. Then I asked how many had been published before, and approximately thirty-eight hands went up. How many had used the article to market their speaking capabilities? Twenty-nine hands went up. How many continue to use the article as a marketing tool? Fourteen hands went up, and so on.

In other words, during my speaking engagement to a group of Washington, DC area speakers, I formulated the basis for a survey-type article entitled "Using Articles to Market Your Speaking Capabilities," which cited actual statistics based on the captive audience I was surveying.

I was similarly able to poll twenty-five Washington, DC area management consultants. These surveys are always of great interest to the press, and this type of information can be submitted as articles or as news releases.

Beyond the Obvious Sources In addition to your local newspapers, a variety of other forums exist that may be interested in printing news about your business. These include community newsletters and shoppers' guides, Chamber of Commerce publications, church bulletins, golf and recreation club newsletters, and health club newsletters.

Several press releases that I have used (and gotten published) are presented on the following pages. The first example announces an annual speaking engagement that I fulfilled for Arlington County's marketing education service. Although the county issues its own news releases for this event, I submit my version to newspapers to get double coverage.

This release follows a generic formula, first mentioning the speaker with a tag line about what he does, what type of session he will be offering, and to whom. This is followed by a little more on the speaker, then the day, date, place, and time the program will be held.

When the information is presented as an announcement, the phone number for more information is always given last. While the examples are for speeches, any set of news releases can follow the same format.

Local Author to Address Arlington Adult Ed Program for Entrepreneurs

Jeff Davidson, certified management consultant and author, will deliver a morning seminar on "Marketing Your Business" for the marketing education service of Arlington County.

Davidson is co-author of *Marketing Your Consulting and Professional Services* (John Wiley), now in its third edition. He is also author of several other books on marketing. Davidson has made 520 presentations in the last 10 years.

The seminar is scheduled for Saturday, February 10, at the Sheraton National Hotel, Columbia Pike and Washington Boulevard, Arlington, Virginia. The program will run from 9 a.m. to 12 noon. For more information, call 328-6930.

The next release represents a variation on the same theme. As you can see, it is the same release, only this time it follows the seminar.

I usually mail this the day of or the day following the actual presentation. Sometimes, a newspaper that did not carry the original release will carry the brief summary of it as a news item. Any publication that does carry the original release, however, is not likely to carry the follow-up release.

Author Addresses Arlington Adult Ed Program for Entrepreneurs

Jeff Davidson, a certified management consultant and author, recently delivered a morning seminar on "Marketing Your Business" for the marketing education service of Arlington County. Davidson is co-author of *Marketing Your Consulting and Professional Services* (John Wiley) and several other books on marketing. The lecture focused on ways to inexpensively but effectively market a professional service.

The next release follows a similar pattern. A speaker is making a presentation to a local group; this time the third paragraph highlights that group. The example printed below is rather brief; a longer one might also be accepted by newspaper editors. Note: I updated my credentials in the release below, which differ slightly from the original release printed by the *Uptown Citizen* and presented on the following page.

Consultant to Speak to Women in Advertising and Marketing

Jeff Davidson, a certified management consultant and author, will address Women in Advertising and Marketing on the topic, "Leveraging Your Professional Relationships to Enhance Your Marketing Efforts."

Davidson is author of *Marketing for the Home-Based Business* (Adams Media), *Marketing Your Consulting and Professional Services*, and *Getting New Clients* (Wiley). He has made 520 presentations to professional groups in the last 10 years.

Women in Advertising and Marketing is an organization composed of female executives in marketing, sales, and communications in the greater Washington area. The organization was formed in May, 1980.

The meeting will take place at the Washington Marriott Hotel at 22nd and M Streets, NW, Washington, DC, and will include a cocktail hour starting at 6 p.m. Dinner is at 7 p.m., followed by Mr. Davidson's presentation at 8 p.m.. For more information, please call 698-4042.

Here is a reprint of my after-the-fact release as it appeared in a weekly community newspaper (Figure 5). I supplied the photograph, which had actually been taken months before and was unconnected to the event.

Author Addresses Women In Advertising

Jeff Davidson

Jeff Davidson, certified management consultant and marketing author addressed Women in Advertising and Marketing on the topic "Leverage Your Professional Relationships to Enhance Your Marketing Efforts." Davidson is co-author of *Marketing Your Consulting and Professional Services* (John Wiley and Sons) which is in its fourth printing in less than 18 months. He is also author of two more books which will be appearing in the spring of 1987 including *Marketing to the Fortune 500* (Dow Jones-Irwin) and *Blow Your Own Horn: How to Market Your Career and Yourelf* (AMACOM Books). He has made over 100 presentations in the last two years.

Women in Advertising and Marketing is an organization composed of female executives in marketing, sales, and communications in the greater Washington area. The organization was established in May 1980 and now enjoys the membership of 225 people.

Davidson is a popular speaker in the Washington, DC area and in the last two years has spoken to over 100 local groups.

Published by The Uptown Citizen, Inc.

4101 River Road, N.W., Washington, D.C. 20016

Whenever you win an award, or are cited for service within your local community or nationally, that represents excellent material for a news release. The release below could also be sent to different groups with different headings targeted for their needs, such as:

"Club Member"
"Small Business Owner"
"Local Resident"
"Business Author"

Author Wins Small-Business Award 5th Year in a Row

For the fifth consecutive year, Jeff Davidson was awarded the U. S. Small Business Administration's Media Advocate of the year for the state of Virginia. The award is given annually to that individual who best serves as an advocate to the general public for the small business community.

During the past year, Davidson's articles in magazines, trade journals, newspapers, and newsletters on topics related to small business reached a combined circulation in excess of 12 million readers.

The award is annually given as part of several festivities held during the second week of May in celebration and observation of National Small Business Week.

"People to Watch"

A variation of the theme of submitting your own home-based press release is to create your own "people to watch" promotion. Many local publications, as well as nationally and internationally distributed magazines including *Forbes* and *Fortune*, have these types of columns. Often they are called by different names such as "Front Runners," "People on the Move," "Movers and Shakers," "Worth Watching," and so forth.

You can't submit these directly to the publications themselves; it appears too self-serving, though *all* business publicity is self-serving. Instead, have this type of publicity ready in case you are asked to submit something about yourself or if those representing you can use it in their efforts.

People to Watch

Jeff Davidson

Since he first discovered portable dictation equipment in October 1979, Jeff Davidson has had more than 3100 articles published on marketing and management. In 1985, he teamed up with Richard A. Connor, Jr. and coauthored *Marketing Your Consulting and Professional Services* (John Wiley), now in its eighth printing in 18 months. Since then he's written twenty-four more books on entrepreneurism, career advancement, and finding breathing space in a sped-up society.

If your appetite for spreading news releases around is sufficiently whetted, here are some suggestions for making an appropriate submission:

- The first time you mention yourself in the release, be sure to spell out your full name, including your middle initial and any title that you use.
- Print the release on clean $8\frac{1}{2}$" × 11" paper, preferably on your letterhead. Place your phone number in the upper left- or right-hand corner, and in the opposite corner spell out when the release may be used, for example, "For Immediate Use" or "For Use During the Week of May 18."
- Follow the journalist's approach to covering news: Tell your readers who, what, where, when, why, and how.

- Write in a simple, straightforward style. The shorter your sentences the better; seventeen words or less per sentence is appropriate for newspapers.
- Send along a photo of yourself (taken in advance). If your release is a professional announcement, a head-and-shoulders shot or an action shot, such as you addressing an audience or visiting a construction site, may grab an editor's attention.
- If you know the name of a particular department or features editor, include it on your outside envelope and on a stick-on note attached to the release. If you are unsure of the proper name, call the switchboard or leave it off. It is better to have no name than the name of someone who has departed.
- Submit only factually accurate releases, including time, date, phone number, etc. The publications to which you submit releases loathe printing items that contain errors.

Realistically, most publications that receive a release will not publish it. Much as with other forms of marketing, you are playing a numbers game here. The smaller the publication and the greater your affiliation with it, as in the case of a professional association newsletter, the more likely it is that your message will be published and seen.

Don't call or write to see if your release is going to be accepted or if it has already been published; you will only be seen as an irritant. In most cases, if your release is published, friends or associates will give you a call.

More of Your Image on Paper: Letters to the Editor

Another opportunity for home-based marketers is the strategy of writing letters to the editor. A published letter to the editor of your local newspaper can be effective as a means of generating publicity.

A published letter to the editor can be reused; simply make an attractive reprint of the letter. Include the date and page, and the logo of the publication in which it appeared with your correspondence to clients and prospects.

The letter to the editor registers a distinct impact with those who read it. It positions you as a responsible, authoritative professional in your field who is taking a leadership and advocacy position on what is presumably an important, current topic.

The key to getting a letter to the editor published in your local newspaper, other than submitting an excellent letter, is speed. Call up the publication in question, inform them that you have a letter to the editor that you would like to send over by fax, and obtain their fax number. The editor in charge of the letters page will appreciate the quick response and, now and then, will even call you back.

Usually, however, your local newspaper receives all of the letters it can handle and selects only a few from a wide field. So don't be disappointed if yours is not chosen. Whereas the competition to get into your local paper may be significant, professional, trade, and industry magazines and journals often go begging when it comes to obtaining thought-provoking letters.

As with other articles and news releases, you need to send your letter to more than one publication. If your local newspaper and a professional journal both want to print the letter, you will have no problem. If two professional journals wish to print the same letter, then withdraw your letter from one of the publications.

THE NAME OF YOUR BUSINESS AFFECTS MARKETING

What business name goes on every piece of literature you disseminate? If you haven't already chosen a name for your business, or if you have one and wish to change it, perhaps to better position yourself, here are some guidelines:

1. *Define your business.* Define your business in its broadest possible terms. If you are a voice coach, you don't simply give voice lessons: you instill confidence in others. Now consider what that makes your service or product stand out from others. What specific features do you offer that others do not? How does your service or product help your customers to save money, accomplish a specific goal, reduce frustration, or save time?

2. *Spell out what you would like your business name to accomplish.* When people hear the name of your business, how will they respond? What vision does the name conjure up? Would the typical, disinterested layperson understand what you do from your business name? Or would you prefer to have an insider's name that will be recognized and appreciated by those who have a high need for your type of service or product? What emotions and feelings, if any, would you like to evoke in others?

3. *Identify and define your target audience.* Specifically, what type of client or customer are you seeking? What is the age, sex, occupation, and socioeconomic status of the typical customer or client? What is the target trying to accomplish? Why will he be attracted to you and your business? Similarly, what qualities of your proposed name will a target find attractive and unattractive? For example, fitness enthusiasts would respond differently to certain words than to others:

Attractive	**Unattractive**
Energizing	Comfortable
Aerobic	Stationary
Trim	Full figured
Physical	Restful

4. *Conduct your own theme search.* Scout your industry or profession and find ten to fifteen company names that you like, admire, or are drawn to, as well as ten to fifteen names that leave you confused, uninspired, or uninterested. Now, focusing on the names that interest you, examine the number of words in each name, the number of syllables, common suffixes or prefixes, sounds, letters, and any other commonalities. Are the names that you are attracted to you:

- Clever—an editorial service called "A Way with Words"
- Straightforward—a Houston-based cellular-phone sales company called "Houston Cellular Phone"
- Rhyming—Corporate relocators called "Residents for Presidents"
- Graphic—A tree-trimming and removal service called "Me & My Chainsaw"

- Cyber—A web graphic designers called "Cyberdesign"
- Descriptive—a word-processing service called "Words on a Page"
- Futuristic—a business and econometric-forecasting service called "TomorrowScope"
- Sensory—a one-person specialty bakeshop called "The Old World Baker"
- A popular catch phrase—a one-woman errand, house-sitting, and odd-jobs service called "Make My Day"

Or do they feed on existing enterprises:

- A variation on a theme—an interior designer for children's nurseries called "Nurseries Я Us"

Strive to create a name that is phonebook friendly, even if you won't be listing it in the phonebook. Names such as "t-1 Graphix," "2-4-1 Window Cleaning," "AArdvark Systems," and others with letter/number combos often confuse customers, are hard to find alphabetically, and may keep you spelling out the name to people all day long. Yes, you can be too clever for your own good.

5. *Try some names on your friends.* Once you have followed steps one through four, a few names may start to emerge. Ask friends, relatives, and associates what they think about the various names you have come up with thus far. For each name that you are testing, consider the following checklist:

- What do they like or not like about it?
- What does the name remind them of, if anything?
- Do they think the name is a good fit for your service, product, or company?
- Can they pronounce the name correctly?
- Can they spell the name correctly?
- Do they get the name confused with any other names?
- Does the name remind them of any other name, or another service, product, or business?
- Can they remember the name easily?
- Do they see the name as consistent with you as an entrepreneur and/or as a company president?

6. *Protect your name.* By now, a single name with which you feel comfortable may emerge. To make sure that your name does not violate any existing trademark, call the Patent and Trademark office of the U. S. Department of Commerce in Washington, DC, 20231, at (202) 557-3061.

You could also hire a trademark and patent attorney to conduct a trade-name search or employ any one of several companies which maintain federal and state trademark databases. Your local librarian will be able to help you find such attorneys or companies.

The Non-Name

Often, the question of what name to choose is immediately solved. Holly Sanders, a licensed clinical social worker (LCSW) based near Atlanta, Georgia, effectively bills herself as Holly Sanders, Licensed Clinical Social Worker. In my own case, Jeff Davidson, MBA, CMC (Certified Management Consultant) was my operating name for several years before I launched the Breathing Space Institute, at *http://www.BreathingSpace.com*

If you have any type of license, certification, or simply a professional title, that makes an adequate business name.

- George Hebron, Electrician
- Carl Mays, Motivator
- Margaret Rutherford, Registered Dietitian
- Dr. Pete Johnson, Strategist
- Paul Dickson, Freelance Writer
- Dr. Marvin Cetron, Futurist
- Robert Hampton, Airport Security Specialist
- Ed Sheppard, Ph.D., Industrial Psychologist
- Rita Rothwarf, Fine Arts Representative
- Juanell Teague, Business Coach of the Future

For the established home-based marketer, selection of the best possible name is not so crucial. If you already have a roster of clients and get a lot of follow-up and referral business, then your existing name is best. If you are in a start-up situation or not well established, selection of an appropriate and fitting name is a more important task.

A good name may capture the imagination and interest of those who might not otherwise call on you. A bad name that connotes an undesirable image can keep customers away. Since having to change a business name can be disruptive, much like having to relocate, don't make the final selection until your small, inner voice says, "Yes!"

Those Key Initials After Your Name

You've seen it on my letterhead: CMC. Your accountant may be a CPA. Your doctor is certainly an M.D., and your lawyer is probably a J.D. One of the ways to enhance your home-based marketing efforts on paper is to obtain professional certification or licensing so that you may add the designated initials after your name on your stationery and all other printed materials.

Certification is a designation voluntarily granted by an association to individuals, usually members of the association, who meet predetermined qualifications. More than 300 associations and professional societies offer professional certification programs in the United States alone. Some of the more commonly known include CPA (Certified Public Accountant), CFP (Certified Financial Planner), CAE (Certified Association Executive), and CMC (Certified Management Consultant).

Licensing is granted by a government body or professional association to individuals who meet predetermined qualifications. In the case of certain professions, such as law, medicine, and dentistry, licensing is required on a state-by-state basis before one can engage in those occupations.

Accreditation is granted by an association to organizations rather than to individuals. Accreditation applies to programs such as those of a college, university, or professional institute that meet predetermined standards through evaluations at the time of application and periodically thereafter.

While many of your prospective clients and customers may have no knowledge of certification programs in your industry and may not know, even when viewing your certification designation (such as CMC), what it stands for, it still subtly signals to them that your abilities and experience meet certain minimum standards.

If you are uncertain whether a certification program is available for the profession or industry in which you do business, two commonly available directories that will help to provide the answer are *Gale's Association Directory* and *National Trade and Professional Associations*. Both are available as reference books in any municipal, college, or subject-specific library.

HOT TIPS/INSIGHTS FROM CHAPTER 3

- Many of the impressions prospects form about your business is based on what they learn about and see of you on paper. So what does your stationery and printed material convey?
- Your business may not require a brochure.
- Nearly every aspect of your business or professional activities can be worked into a news release. Always be on the lookout for news-release items.
- Writing letters to the editor can be a quick way to gain publicity.
- If you are in the startup phase, choose your business name carefully and after considerable thought. If you are already established, change your business name if you have evidence that it is disruptive to your overall marketing efforts.
- Seek certification; many people have no idea what certification means, but they like the sound of it and will forgive you for working from your home if you are a certified professional.

CHAPTER 4

Marketing Online

Think of the World Wide Web as an information guide-book and advertising directory with 60,000,000 entries that are updated or changed every picosecond.

If you're considering marketing online, you first have to ask yourself, are your prospective customers there? Increasingly, for home-based marketers in every field, the answer is "Yes!"

Who has been visiting the Web, however? Obviously any figures I offer will change markedly with each passing day. As of the late 1990s, Internet users had an average salary of $59,000, compared to the U. S. average of $20,690. According to *One Source*, the average age was 33 years old.

Why do people use the Web? Based on findings in *What Makes People Click*, by NetSmart, 97% of users want to be better informed, 81% want to research product and service information, with a large percentage becoming buyers, and 57% surf the Web for fun. What about the average bookmarks per user? Based on a survey of 17,000 users by Georgia Institute of Technology, 18% of users bookmark 1 to 10 items, 39% bookmark 11 to 50 items, 19% bookmark 51 to 100 items, and 19% bookmark more than 100.

Forget everything else you've heard or read. At the minimum, quite simply, having a good Web site has become standard business practice, like having a fax machine. You can also reduce your need for printing, copying, faxing, and mailing marketing materials once you're able to convey the same information to interested parties via the Web.

Why Is the Web Different?

"Every other kind of marketing prior to the Web has been 'push,'" says Web guru David Arnold, Ph.D. He is coauthor with Gail Rutman of *Business on the Internet: The Concise Handbook* (http://www.daspeaks.com).

"Direct mail, print and broadcast media advertising, telemarketing, billboards—they all involve *pushing* information at people. The message reaches an intended market and has an impact whether the communication is welcomed or not.

"You probably didn't choose to memorize the McDonald's slogan you deserve a break today—the push model of marketing burned it into your awareness nonetheless," says Arnold. "So putting a billboard on the asphalt highway works. Putting it on the Information Highway doesn't. You have to draw visitors to your information. This means even the world's best site will have no impact unless you pull people into it." Too much of the Web is self-serving hype about the Web itself. There are too many people seeking to prove to everyone that they know how to make "cool" graphics.

USING THE WEB FOR HOME-BASED MARKETING

The Internet was designed to be an information distribution system. The Web in particular gives you the leverage to deliver value faster and better than ever before, but only if your Web site focuses on your customers and not on making you feel good about your venture. Ron Wagner, a web designer, consultant, and trainer in Herndon, Virginia, says, "When your Internet site becomes a focal point and distribution system for valuable information, Internet users will find it, use it, return to it, and tell others about it."

The marketing task has changed from pushing your home-based business and its goods and/or services to pulling your customer into value-added opportunities that you provide. This marketing change, says marketing guru Richard Connor, CMC, is profound, as in changing from "checkers to chess—the play and strategy are different and more complex. In fact, it's even more of a change than that because you don't even use the same old board in this new game."

Wagner, who has written dozens of specialized Internet guides (for information visit: http://www.citapei.com), observes that all the buzz these days about audio, video, and action-packed JavaScripts can distract a home-business marketer who wants to use the Web for marketing from doing it effectively. The typical core strategic goals for the home-based entrepreneurs (HBEs) on the Internet include:

- To create a Web site for delivering information that your customers will regard as valuable, creating a Web site that becomes the "gift that keeps on giving" to its visitors
- To continually increase the promotion and delivery of items of value to your key customers and prospects, as defined by them
- To promote your business

Customer-Centered Interneting

Richard Connor says that a basic principle in using the Web is that your customers or prospects *must feel that they earn a suitable return on their time investment in visiting your Web site.* You only get an initial 10 to 20 seconds to convince visitors that you offer value in return for their time.

Web site visitors will judge your site based on how it delivers perceived value. People will sell themselves based on how much your Web site improves their lives or their business. "Even if you don't surf the Net much yourself," says Wagner, "you probably have enjoyed its amazing abilities to deliver previously obscure or hard-to-locate information. The prime goal for your Web site is to help your customers find information that consistently will add value to their lives and companies."

So ask yourself, what information can you distribute via the Internet that:

Develop an Insider's Understanding

An important tool for the customer-centered Interneter is to possess an "insider's understanding" of the business, environments, and expectations of your customers. Richard Connor asserts that once you have an "insider's understanding" of your customers' needs, you can raise issues that demand their attention and likewise use your web site to further your efforts. You can then include links to sites that offer or discuss solutions.

"Constantly check out your customers' Web sites as well as the Web sites of their competitors," says Ron Wagner. You don't have to find everything by searching. Many Web features help you build an "insider's understanding" within your targeted niches automatically. For example, subscribing to newsgroups and mailing lists that affect customers is a fundamental, easy way to stay informed. A good place to start on this quest is with the DejaNews search engine at http://www.dejanews.com

Also, you can save visitors from the over-information crunch. The effects that over-information has on people actually can work in favor of your home-based business. You can provide a valuable service to your Web site visitors by sorting and repackaging information and then providing links to the information they most need or want to see.

This repackaging can give customers a safe haven where they know they quickly can tap into a minuscule portion of information that they actually need, the key information you can provide.

1. Enhances performance
2. Improves profits
3. Improves the customer's working environment

Wagner says, "You may believe we all work in a cold, impersonal business world, but even in cyberspace people make most decisions by intuition. They then justify a buying decision to themselves and to others by the use of such things as competitive proposals and testimonials that support their decision."

While an ingenious, humorous, or attractive Web site may draw a slew of first-time curiosity seekers, no one will return often if they discover no perceived value for them at your site.

Test Visitors

This is so easy to do, yet so rarely done among home-based marketers online: induce people to visit your site. You want allies to give you the critical input you need to make your site more appealing and useful and visited more often. It is hard to be the sole judge of your own Web site's effectiveness. *The more input you get from your target market, the greater your objectivity will be.* Consider asking:

1. *Previous and current clients.* Ask anyone in the industry who will be responsive as well. These are key sources of feedback. Treat them well.
2. *Peers.* Ask other HBEs, for they can help enormously. In particular, ask those who do not compete with you.
3. *Web Specialists.* They can tell you things you wouldn't have heard elsewhere. Many are techno-types with no flair for design; some have the whole package knowledge of html, java, CIG, Perl, and a tremendous sense of how to build an attractive, eye-catching site that people will want to revisit.

What do you ask your test visitors? Here are some ideas:

- Did the site load quickly enough for you?
- Was it visually appealing?
- Were you able to navigate about easily?

- Are the photos and icons appropriate?
- What feature did you like best?
- What feature did you like least?
- How does it compare with other sites?
- What would you like to see?
- What would make you return?
- What else can you suggest?

If some of your targets are overseas, sweep through your site to make sure that an international visitor will have an easy time navigating your site as well. Then ask people who are key contacts to be test visitors. You'd be amazed how some people are utterly flattered by this, while, of course, others won't respond at all.

Build a Gift That Keeps on Giving

Much of the valuable information you post on your Web site is likely to be time-sensitive. The value visitors find today may be worthless next week. This is not to say you can't post useful and static information. My site, http://www.BreathingSpace.com, for example, includes a feature called "Book Digest," where nearly one hundred books are summarized. Visitors may download a digest note of their choice for free. I do add to the book digest periodically, but basically it is a static portion of my Web site. If some of the information you provide on the Internet is static, then you can post it and simply leave it in place. Note: see page 69 for winning strategies that get visitors to return to your site.

Whether static or dynamic, visitors who find worthwhile information on their first visit to your site are much more likely to return. If they find the same information on the second visit, most still will visit again. Wagner advises that three visits to the same old page probably is the limit; at that point you may lose a prospect forever. Perhaps some users may give you another look in a few months, but maybe not.

Hook'em by Various Means

To find a product, service, or simply information on the Web, most people usually head straight for one or more of the online search engines and request a key word search. "When these

Web-site seekers submit key words related to your business," says David Arnold, "you need to make sure that yours is one of the Web sites that comes up on screen."

Arnold warns that entering one or a set of key words will bring up thousands of sites. If your site doesn't appear in the first few screenfuls displayed, on say Yahoo or Lycos, it might as well not be there at all. Web surfers will find someone else's site first and will never see that yours exists.

So your task is to make sure that the search engines have your site listed and that you rise to the top of the listings.

"Some search engines scour the Web," Arnold says, "locating and indexing new sites as they appear." Others, like Yahoo! (http://www.yahoo.com), list only those sites that are submitted to them. To get listed, you have to go to their site, click on their "add URL" button, and fill in their registration form. These forms can be long and tedious, but if you want to be in the world's largest directories, stay with it.

Arnold suggests *manually registering your site even with the search engines that would list it automatically*. "Each search engine operates differently. Some index only home pages; others the entire site," Arnold says. "For those pages they do index, some search engines catalog every word on the page, some only the title, and others fall somewhere in between. If you don't have the words a visitor is searching for in your site, and more specifically in the part of the site the given search engine indexes, the prospective visitor will never find you. So you need to feed the right words to each search engine by registering your site yourself."

To optimize your listing, Arnold says to consider registering more than just your home page. Many agencies appear online to handle search engine registration for site owners, usually for a fee. Yahoo maintains a list of agencies at: http://www.yahoo.com/ Business_and_Economy/Companies/Internet_Services/Web_ Presence_Providers/Announcement_Services.

Arnold observes that the old maxim "if you want a thing done well, do it yourself" has never been truer than when listing your Web site in search engines. A free service that isn't in the Yahoo list, called Submit-It, http://www.submit-it.com, can be quite helpful in enabling you to register with many search engines.

Another company, called Power Solutions, has developed (http://www.sitepromoter.com), a site which eases much of the pain of do-it-yourself search engine registration. "The program contains links to the top fifty promotional search engines, as well as to a secondary set of one hundred general business promotional engines," says Arnold. "And the software supplies you with a detailed registration form, from which it automatically pulls the right information for each search engine."

Say the magic words

A few search engines give you an indication of the criteria they use for ranking the sites that come up in a search. Arnold cautions that none give you anywhere near the information you need to optimize your positioning. The answers, he says, are at http://zuww.calafia.com/webmasters, "A Webmaster's Guide to Search Engines." This online guide includes articles on how each of the most popular search engines works, a chart comparing the data, and tips for giving your site the best possible position in the results line. Voilà!

After you determine how the individual search engines operate, your task becomes one of tailoring your submission material to match each one—http://www.SitePromoter.com (or Site Promoter) actually handles some of this task for you.

To test the results of your efforts, Ron Wagner suggests that you periodically revisit the search engines, entering the kind of words your customers or prospects might use in the search for a business likes yours, and see if your site emerges! If your site is on the opening screen, great job. "If you're languishing on the Web floor," Arnold sympathizes, "figure out why, and resubmit your information."

The Tom Sawyer Effect—Getting Others to Promote Your Site

Not all visits to your Web site come by way of search engines. Effective home-based web marketers increasingly need to develop special relationships, "strategic alliances," as Richard Connor calls them, "both with organizations and individuals with whom they jointly serve the needs of customers." Can you cross-link with related sites? Once you establish special, cross-linked relation-ships, your task, he says, is jointly to sense, sell, serve, and satisfy the needs and expectations of mutual customers who visit your site and the site to whom you're linked.

"Clicking into your site from a link on another site serves a special purpose," Arnold says. "It makes the visit to you an *impulse purchase* of sorts, like picking up a magazine or candy bar while standing in line at the supermarket checkout counter. The impulse visit creates *anticipation of a profitable experience*, since that link to you on another person's site *implies a recommendation* of you and your services."

To get others to link to you, simply ask them. If your site pro-vides great value to visitors then for some sites which you're trying to link with, linking is, indeed, an easy way for them to increase the value they're giving their visitors. Arnold says to send them an e-mail and explain your view. You just might get a yes.

I'll scratch your back
Arnold recommends offering an incentive to those who link your site from theirs—you link back to them. "Only do this, how-ever, if linking to another site will add to your marketing image and position," warns Arnold. "Every time you provide an external link, you push your customers out your door. Make sure the site you're sending them to will give you value in return."

- The best sites to link with are related to, but don't compete with, your business.
- Link with suppliers, related industries, even customers.
- Link with those who are connected in some way with what you do.

"Y'all Come Back Now!"
It's one thing to a have a web that is attractive and eye-catching; it's quite another thing to develop a site that is not only informative, but that induces visitors to *keep coming back and leads to business*. Here are a variety of winning strategies:

1. *Periodic Updates.* Change something on your opening screen once a week. Change topics, availability, products,

and services as warranted. If you don't change your site regularly, some people will assume that you have nothing new to offer (perish the thought!).

2. *Up-to-the-Minute Updates.* Preempt your competition by offering the latest on a topic of interest to your targets, including trends, breakthroughs, meeting results, etc. If you are so inclined and have the resources, you could position your site as the place to visit each day for late-breaking industry news. Alternatively, offer rotating public service messages.

3. *Quickly Engaging.* Encourage immediate participation. Give visitors a choice. Engage them. For example, have them pick door A or B, answer a preliminary question, choose from a list, vote for something, or send in their opinion.

4. *Visitors Bonuses.* Author and publisher Roger Herman, CMC, says to offer them something if they give their names and addresses.

5. *Tip of the Day, Week, Month.* I offer a thought for the day and a weekly tip sheet of new ways to have more Breathing Space (http://www.BreathingSpace.com). Scott Adams and his syndicators offer last Sunday's Dilbert strip (http://www.unitedmedia.com/comics/dilbert/).

6. *Online Tutorial.* Teach your visitors something; offer short, to-the-point instructions or guidance on something that is of interest or will be widely appreciated.

7. *For Members Only.* Offer features that are for "members" only: one needs a password to enter. You could offer the same type of exclusivity by issuing passwords only to visitors who have logged in, sent e-mail, and so forth.

8. *Visitors' Comments.* David Arnold (http://www.david arnold.com) says, "Post comments from your e-mail or other communication, such as the increasingly popular online guest book. Include only relevant excerpts that say something specific about you, your business, or your products and services."

9. *Groupware.* California attorney Rita Risser (http://www.fairmeasure.com) says, "I completed a 6-month groupware project. It's an effective way to impart informa-

tion and also can generate powerful emotional connections. Groupware is like a chat room. Let's say I have twenty-five learning points. Each point would be a thread. I might start a topic with a case study, and then people would respond, reading earlier responses and building on them. Or I might ask a question such as 'What does sexual harassment mean to you?' and then facilitate the discussion."

10. *On this Day.* What happened on this date 100, 50 or 25 years ago? Whose birthday is it? (Especially use the birthday of someone prominent in speaking/meetings/bureaus and such.) What else about "this day" can you offer to daily visitors?

11. *This Week's Winner.* Pose a question. The following week, announce the winner on your Web site, reward the winner, and pose a new question. Use e-mail, ads, lists, and other P.R. to get participants.

12. *100th or 1000th Visitor Awards.* If you collect visitors' e-mail addresses at your site, you could give an award for each 100th or 1000th visitor.

In short, think of all the things you could offer at your site, a little bit at a time. For example:

- A series of articles, once a week or at some other interval.
- Survey or polling results, especially if it builds or changes each week.
- A running commentary on the news or events in your specialty area.
- Rating guide to products or services, such as hotels, airlines, airports, a/v equipment, and such.
- Review service: of books, software, programs, courses, the Web, etc. All of those "cool sites of the day" are nothing more than attempts to win repeat visitors.

Promote Your Site Off-line

Prospective customers can find out about you online as well as off-line. Many of the same tactics for marketing any product or service apply to marketing your Web site. David Arnold advises promoting your Web site address on all your other marketing tools: business cards, stationery, print and other media advertising, brochures, press releases, and anything else that carries your physical address, phone number, and e-mail address.

TOP 10 TIPS FOR A SUCCESSFUL WEB SITE

To close the chapter, here are some of Ron Wagner's ideas on ten of the best customer-centered strategies you can apply to your Web site, presented in ascending order:

1. *Keep visitors from getting lost.* Ensure that every page on your site includes multiple links that take them back to your home page, to the previous page, or to another value-packed page. If visitors get lost or side-tracked while exploring your site, you don't want them to move on to another site out of frustration. Ensure that they can quickly return to something familiar and comfortable or move forward to something that will bring them value.

2. *Go easy on the graphics.* Thousands of Web sites are works of art by master graphic artists. During peak business hours, however, some people may not be able to access your site. Use small graphics and offer a "text-only" hyperlink on the home page so that visitors can select a faster option if they can't wait for your art to download.

3. *Include multiple contact links.* It is a waste of your time and resources if a visitor decides to contact you and can't locate the necessary information. Some highly professional-looking sites contain no contact links. People want personal contact and cyberspace hasn't changed that. In fact, a personal touch on your site may heighten people's interest.

    Your site should contain an obvious link that points visitors to personal contact information within your organization: e-mail, fax, snail mail address and phone numbers, if appropriate.

4. *Test it personally.* Test your site to see how it looks and feels to customers. Use different settings (toolbars and

directory buttons on and off); different hours (lunchtime and evening); different modems (slow and fast); different browsers (Internet Explorer, Netscape, and Macintosh, if possible); different screen resolutions. You may be quite happy with your site's performance on a fast Pentium PC with a top-of-the-line graphics card, but then be surprised when you see it on an older, slower PC with a slow modem. Different visitors are going to have different experiences.

5. *Build it with professional designers.* If you're not a Web design whiz, and the chances are high that you're not, get help! Investing in a professional designer and ad copywriters may be an excellent business investment, if you can afford it. Or, find a college whiz kid who'll appreciate the extra earnings.

6. *Submit it to indexers and directories.* As mentioned, contact every major Web indexer, especially Yahoo!, Lycos, AltaVista, and Excite, and make sure you're listed, or get listed.

7. *Link, link, link.* Cut deals with everyone you can whose site relates to your business. Get your link on as many other pages as possible. Of course, you will reciprocate. Multiple links make your site more valuable because your customers will know that you are a source for fresh, worthwhile, related sites from all over the Web.

8. *Preview regularly scheduled updates.* Include on your site a preview listing of upcoming topics. You never know when a visitor might find nothing at your site today, but notices something important in the preview that will bring him back next week.

9. *Start now and grow.* Any moderately advanced user of WordPerfect or Word quickly can create some basic web pages. Get the site up and running and let the search engines start indexing your keywords.

10. *Make it customer-centered.* Focus on the needs of others. Make sure that your most valuable information has the most direct access with the fewest graphics. Provide value that rewards your visitors, and they will reward you. If you concentrate on nothing else, making your site customer

oriented will place you at the head of the class. Remember, a good Web site is never done; update it often.

HOT TIPS/INSIGHTS FROM CHAPTER 4:

- Make your Internet site a focal point and distribution system for valuable information so that Internet users will find it, use it, return to it, and tell others about it.
- Continually ponder what information you can distribute via the Internet that enhances performance, improves profits, or improves your customer's working environment.
- Manually register your site, *even with the search engines that would list it automatically.*
- Ask others to link to you. If your site provides great value to visitors, then for some sites with whom you seek linkage, adding your site will be an easy way for them to increase the value they're giving their visitors.
- Promote your Web site address on all your other marketing tools: business cards, stationery, print and other media advertising, brochures, press releases, and anything else that carries your mailing address, phone number, and e-mail address.
- Make sure that your Web site focuses on the needs of the people you seek to serve.

CHAPTER 5

We're So Glad You Called

Every time your phone rings you have the opportunity
to powerfully and profoundly impact the caller to
develop a bond that could result in mutual prosperity
or to never call you again.

The people who call to inquire about your products or services are the single most valuable commodity in the long-term prosperity of your enterprise. Hence you need to *"give good phone"*; otherwise you may be turning business away.

The key issue in using the phone as a home-based marketer is to recognize that the phone is a tool; nothing more, nothing less. Similar to other tools that you use, such as a computer, copier, or fax machine, it requires following certain procedures. To be the best you can be on the phone you have to be relaxed. You want your call to convey a professional, even-paced, upbeat message. So, you never want to make calls when you're tired, have just received bad news, are time-pressured, or otherwise preoccupied.

Unfortunately, the telephone still represents one of the weak links in the marketing chain for the home-based marketer. Some of the more common usage problems include:

- Answering too quickly or indistinctly
- Not having a consistent phone greeting

- Not having an adequate telephone-answering service
- Not fully capitalizing on calls that represent new business

To Answer, Perchance to Greet

Being on the phone is a full-time activity in and of itself. However, being on the phone and staring out the window, fiddling with items on your desk, or otherwise distracting yourself generally will diminish your capacity to market your services.

Many home-based entrepreneurs report that one of the reasons they left the traditional office was to get away from unnecessary meetings, phone calls, and other interruptions. Regardless of what type of phone services you employ, there will be times where you may end up answering the phone yourself. Let's start then with an exploration of caller greetings.

One Telephone Line Only

There is one primary situation when it's permissible and perhaps practical to maintain one phone line serving as both your business and your personal line—when you live alone, if no one else is in the house during your work day, or if you are the only one who answers the phone. (If you're online for more than 30 minutes a day, receiving many e-mail or fax messages, or otherwise tying up your only line, then you need a second line, and maybe a third.)

The best greeting clearly states your company's name, e.g., Joe Smith Consulting. Those who regularly call you will come to know that during business hours you answer your phone for business callers.

Some people answer with, "Joe Smith Consulting. How can I help you?" or simply "May I help you?" both of which *lack punch*. Dave Yoho, whose letterhead you saw earlier, says that answering with a routine greeting may deliver a message to others that you are not interested in helping them. This is because overused phrases eventually become devoid of meaning. Yoho recommends showing appreciation for the caller, for example, "Thank you for calling Joe Smith Consulting," or even, "Thanks for calling Joe Smith Consulting. How may I help you today?"

Home-based business notwithstanding, if most of your calls are not from prospective clients and you prefer to answer with a traditional "Hello," it's acceptable to do so if you follow an effective dialogue sequence, such as the following:

> The phone rings; you pick it up and say "Hello."
>
> The other party says, "Joe Smith?" "I'd like to speak to Joe Smith," "Is this Joe Smith Consulting?," or "Is Joe Smith there?"
>
> The preferred response in this situation is *"Speaking!"* in a vibrant, upbeat tone.

By responding with "Speaking!" following "hello," you set up the other party to launch into his quest. Invariably he will respond with something like one of these:

- "My name is so and so and I am calling to..."
- "Are you the Joe Smith who..."
- "I am trying to find out if..."
- "Someone told me that you..."

From any of these prompts, you can then launch into a standard business conversation. If you are otherwise effective from that point on, you lose few points overall by initially answering with "Hello."

Two or More Phone Lines

If you have at least one phone line solely for business, then the appropriate greeting is "Joe Smith Consulting" or, as Dave Yoho recommends, "Thank you for calling Joe Smith Consulting." Everyone who hears that greeting knows who they've reached.

High-Powered Telephone Responsiveness

Whether you're answering your own phone or someone is answering for you, here are some guidelines that will yield the greatest long-term marketing results.

- Always answer slowly and clearly so that each syllable in your company name is distinguishable. "Joe Smith Consulting" said too quickly can sound like, "Joce Mitkin Sulting." A rushed greeting, particularly a rushed expression of your company's name, signals to many callers that you rush your work.

- Treat every call as if it is from a major client or customer. Never discount the business potential of a caller because he has a diminutive voice or does not follow the same line of conversation or questioning used by other callers. If you employ an answering service (more on this below), it is particularly important to convey how you want each call to be answered and each caller to be treated.

- Answer the call by the second or third ring. Answering the call on the first ring is acceptable, although some people may be startled and need time to adjust. Answering after the fourth ring can annoy callers and also convey the message that you are under-resourced, although these days most callers are pleased simply when they do not have to listen to endless rounds of voice mail instructions.

- Answer with a smile. Though callers can't see your smile, they can certainly "hear" it in your voice. Your attitude and temperament come through loud and clear over the phone lines. As a home-based marketer, your goal when you answer the phone is to present a voice that projects enthusiasm, success, and quiet confidence.

- Make the caller feel glad he called by conveying interest and enthusiasm.

- Always introduce yourself regardless of whether he has introduced himself, i.e., "This is Joe Smith speaking."

- Let the caller voice his or her concerns and ask his or her questions in their entirety, even if you know the answer before he has finished speaking. Show interest in his problem. It has been said that "Callers don't care how much you know, until you show how much you care."

- Use the caller's name. The very second that the caller tells you his or her name, write it down. Also begin taking notes as he speaks. As you respond to what he is saying, intermittently use his name and any key words or phrases that he has used.

- Ask questions. All things being equal, the longer a caller stays on the line with you, the higher the probability that he will do business with you. Ask questions as a means of lengthening the duration of conversations and gleaning the data necessary to both serve the client's needs and reflect your capabilities.

Too many home-based marketers are overeager to list the services or capabilities that they can offer. An effective questioning process, however, conveys to a caller that you were the right person to call and that he made a good decision in dialing your number.

A SIMPLE SOLUTION: THE ANSWERING MACHINE

Everyone who may call you has confronted voice mail and answering machines and hence is usually ready to leave a message if he or she so desires. If your phone system offers an optional number of rings before it answers, set it on the first or second ring. This shortens callers' overall throughput time and minimizes disruption if you are present but not interested in answering the phone.

Suppose you're willing to answer the phone but frequently leave your desk? In that case, set the answering machine or voice mail system to pick up on four rings, so that you have enough time to answer when you choose, but the device will automatically answer when you are not there in time.

Your message, much as when you answer the phone yourself, needs to be clear, upbeat, and to the point. Don't clutter your message with greeting baggage such as "We are not here right now."

Never leave a message that momentarily cons callers into thinking you're present, such as "This is Joe Smith," followed by a pause long enough to sucker callers into speaking to what they believe is Joe Smith live, followed by, "I'm not in right now, but if you leave a message..." This irritates most callers and convinces some to hang up on the spot, never to call again.

Unless you're in show business, don't use musical or theatrical messages. Don't use celebrity voice greetings or any other device that prompts callers to question the wisdom of their calling you.

If you use a voice mail system, keep the options simple and short. If a caller has to listen to more than three options, you may lose him. This is especially true if the caller had hoped to reach you more easily because it's a home-based business.

Don't use voice mail options to make it sound if you're a large company. You can fool all of the callers, perhaps, one time. You can fool a few callers more than once. After that, everyone can discern that you're using voice mail to convey something that you're not or simply to hide.

What to say
Here is a potpourri of effective messages:

- "You have reached Joe Smith Consulting. Office hours are from 9 to 5:30 p.m. At the tone, please leave your name and number and a brief message."
- "You have reached 953-5601, Joe Smith Consulting. Please leave your name, number, and message and we will call you back between _____ and _____."
- "This is the voice of Joe Smith, president of Joe Smith Consulting. At the tone you'll have up to 2 minutes to leave your message."
- "Thank you for calling Joe Smith Consulting. Your message is important. Please respond at the sound of the tone."
- "You've reached Joe Smith Consulting. At the tone please leave your name and number and a message of any length you desire."

Here are some of the basic marketing advantages and disadvantages of telephone answering machines and voice mail systems:

Advantages
- The public is familiar with telephone answering devices.
- Most systems offer options to fit your needs.
- You maintain complete control over the message given.
- Some callers prefer being able to unload a long message knowing it will be fielded by you.
- Many callers appreciate being able to leave a message at any time.
- They are relatively inexpensive.

- They are relatively repair-free.
- No additional expenses.

Disadvantages

- Some people who will respond to an answering service operator may not respond to a telephone answering machine or to voice mail.
- Ultimately your system will convey an impression of a small or home-based business, a disadvantage if you wish to avoid projecting that image.
- If the tape malfunctions, you can miss several calls and have no clue as to who called. If the voice mail system confuses callers or doesn't provide a logical sequence of options, you may irritate or lose callers.
- Callers who leave messages too quickly force you to replay the message repeatedly to decipher it.

Answering systems today come in a wide variety of shapes and sizes, packages, and options. You will want the following standard features to support your home-based marketing efforts.

Recommended Standard Features

- *Remote message check.* You need the capability of remote calling or checking in. Most systems allow you to remotely receive messages, clear the messages, change your outgoing message, or perform a combination of any of the above.
- *Two-way recording.* With a few simple steps, some systems can record your conversations with others. When you wish to record both your voice and the voice of the caller, a built-in capacity requires only a few simple steps. Note: to avoid potential legal complications, tell the other party that you are taping.
- *Monitor in/out.* When you work at home and don't wish to be disturbed, the "monitor out" feature enables you to continue working while the system silently answers the phone, takes the message, and resets itself.

If you own a combination telephone and answering machine, or have a voice mail system, here are other features that will support your home-based marketing efforts:

- Memory, speed dialing
- Hold button
- Automatic redial
- Speaker phone, useful if you make conference calls to include other people in the room with you. (Note: some people dislike the "speaking from a box" sound of speaker phones. Soon enough, new speaker phones that don't sound like speaker phones will be available.)

Optional Features

Other options with which you are probably familiar include:

- Call waiting. *Not recommended* for home-based entrepreneurs with one phone line. With the rise of speed dial and automatic redial features, many people trying to reach you today have little problem redialing if your line is busy. Also, call waiting can cause many problems with other equipment tied into your systems such as a modem. Surveys indicate that many callers rate call waiting as the single most irritating capability they encounter when calling another party.

  Pacific Bell was considering me to be a spokesperson for their phone services, including call waiting for business. I maintained that it was stress-inducing, unprofessional, unproductive, and deleterious to marketing. They chose someone else to be their spokesperson.

- Call forwarding. Useful when you need to receive a phone call at an outside location. When you move around frequently and others could end up fielding your messages, call forwarding represents telephone overkill.

- Three-way calling. Useful in negotiating and closing deals with two or more other parties. Saves a great deal of back-and-forth calling.

- Repeat call. Your phone keeps attempting a busy number for up to thirty minutes while letting you make other calls. Once the line sought becomes available, your phone rings you and places the call. If you are in the middle of another conversation, you hear a brief tone that signals that the other line is now clear.

A variety of other services, such as call blocking, call tracing, and caller identification have long been available, and some are certainly interesting, but considering the practical side of marketing from home, none are necessary.

Call blocking is useful if you receive numerous unwanted calls from the same parties. Call tracing is a godsend if you receive harassing or abusive calls. Caller I.D. also provides benefits under many scenarios. Nevertheless, if you can do without any of these, you will save time and money.

USING THE YELLOW PAGES

A few years back, a research group called more than 5,000 Yellow Pages advertisers and said, "I saw your ad in the Yellow Pages. How much does it cost [for the product or service offered]?"

The response statistics were outrageous. More than 78% never asked for the caller's name. Over 55% took more than eight rings to answer. Over 42% said the price but then listed other products and services without gauging the caller's interest. Other atrocities revealed in this experiment are reflected in these responses:

"We don't advertise in the Yellow Pages."
"I don't know, can you call back when the boss is here?"

Rapid speech, so that it was difficult to determine the name of the company or division, characterized many of the responses. Lack of enthusiasm, anxiety, or lack of empathy was also evident on many calls. Fewer than 10% answered the phone in a courteous, professional manner and made the callers feel as if they wanted their business.

Granted, most of the companies were not home-based entrepreneurs. Nevertheless, these findings give you some idea of how misused the phone and a Yellow Page ad can be. Your decision to place an ad in the Yellow Pages is based on a few key factors:

- Is your prospect likely to consult the Yellow Pages in the first place?
- Will your ad generate enough revenue to more than justify the expense, and will it help position you in the minds of those you wish to serve?

If so, you probably need to place an ad.

Most people who refer to the Yellow Pages are contemplating using a service or buying a product. They mean business, and now they are deciding whom to call. To your advantage, representatives from the Yellow Pages directories in your area may work directly with you, helping you design your ads and supplying you with data on the people who use their directories. Ninety percent of Yellow Pages advertising space is sold to local businesses.

Developing an Effective Yellow Pages Ad

Here are some tips for developing an effective Yellow Pages advertisement that supports your overall marketing efforts:

- Think from the reader's point of view. For your business, does the customer need more than the telephone number? Hours of operation? Location? A map? Make it easy for the reader to find you. A local landmark may help: "Two blocks west of King's Drug Store."
- Distinguish your business from the competition. Are your years in business important to customers? Do you accept credit cards?
- Keep the ad clean and simple.
- Avoid using your company name as the heading unless it is descriptive.
- Stick to two typefaces.
- Use bullet points.

Your Ad's Purpose

What do you want the ad to accomplish for you? Do you want it to make you appear more substantial than you are? Do you want it to create an image (e.g., of high quality, individualized service, convenience, low prices)?

With your own purpose in mind, review other advertisements that seem to serve similar purposes. What is it about this ad that works? What is it about that one that gives it a high-class image? Why did my eye fall on this one before all the others in its category?

- The Directory Heading. Under which heading should your company name appear? Public relations counselors can be listed under "Advertising Agencies and Counselors." The company listed under "Home Improvements" can also be listed under "Electricians," "Plumbers," and "Roofing Contractors."
- Providing General Information. You'll need to provide enough information to give your business some appeal and interest, but not so much that nobody wants to read it all. Readers of Yellow Pages advertisements want to know your name, location, phone number, e-mail address or Web site, acceptance of credit cards or other convenience factors—the basics—and a few of the most outstanding features about your business. The outstanding features include information that you think will draw customers: "no waiting" or "next to the subway stop."
- Color and Pictures. Some use of color can be eye-catching, but it often serves to clutter an ad and leave the reader not knowing where to look first. Pictures, which may be drawings or photographs, have the same effect.
- Type Styles and Sizes. When you scan the Yellow Pages, think about what styles of type catch your eye. How big is the type that draws your attention, especially in ads the same size as yours will be? Strive for a clean, readable look, with your company name in a type that is bolder than the rest of the type in your ad and at least twice as large.

Your Ad's Copy

When you're writing the advertisement, you will be concerned with the ad heading, copy for your ad, the inclusion of your company's name, address, and telephone number, and the use of artwork that will reinforce your sales message. Here is some of the vital information you'll want to include:

- Year Established. When a consumer sees that your business has been around for a while, he will feel more secure about using it, home office or not. It's hard to argue with "in business since 1983" or "four years in the same location."
- Delivery/Pick-up. Let your customers know how you are willing to satisfy their needs and fit their schedules.
- Convenient Hours. Accent your availability.
- Free Estimates. Before consumers make a commitment, they want to know exactly what they are in for. If you provide an expensive service, a free estimate will work to your advantage by giving the customer a sense of security and control.

Effective ad copy contains at least a few of the features listed below:

- The Ad Heading. The heading on your ad needs to draw attention to your business. A strong heading helps catch people's eyes when they're searching through the Yellow Pages.
- Distinguishing Copy. Tell customers what services you offer, and distinguish yourself from your competitors with phrases such as "family-run business" or "We guarantee everything we sell."
- White Space. The amount of space within your ad that is not taken up by type or artwork is important. White space prevents a cluttered look. Look for ads that are the same size as the one you plan to place and see how much white space is used in the ones that catch your eye.
- Artwork. Use line drawings that relate to your product or service. Make sure they are clear and simple so they will reproduce well in the printing process.

Beyond Traditional Yellow Pages

Many mini-Yellow Pages exist today. These are small directories, ¼" thick or less, focusing on a specific locale. Advertising in mini-Yellow Pages offer both advantages and disadvantages:

Advantages
- More attractive cost. Many of the independent publishers offer advertising rates averaging 30% to 40% below those of the larger phone conglomerates.
- More flexibility. Your ad will not be constrained by the more stringent dictates of the larger publishers.
- Ad development help. While the big Yellow Pages will provide sales representatives to help you develop your ad, the smaller ones will give you more personalized attention without the pressure to run a larger ad.
- Local orientation. Community directories deal more effectively with the needs of nearby residents.
- Better grade of paper. Because these books are smaller, their paper is often heavier and sturdier. This makes the book more attractive to a customer who does not want to deal with ripped, flyaway pages.
- General information section. This category includes any information about the community that will add to the convenience and utility of the book: such items as maps, public transportation guides, special-events calendars, and schedules of local sports teams.

Disadvantages
- In many communities, mini-Yellow Pages are not well established. So, no matter how little you pay for an ad, you may be overspending.
- Distribution may be poor.
- It is unclear whether people retain them.

Is an 888 or 877 Number in Your Future?

If 10% to 20% or more of your revenue is derived from clients or customers outside your local calling area, you may want to install toll-free telephone service. Any long-distance carrier can provide you with 888 or 877 service (the 800 series has been consumed) to your home-based office.

In many surveys, respondents indicate that they always call companies first that advertise a toll-free number. One variety of toll-free 888 or 877 telephone service allows callers from across the nation to place orders or make inquiries by calling your toll-free line, which is answered by a commercial service. Such companies often offer a complete range of services such as:

- Database development
- Inbound telephone service
- Telemarketing fulfillment
- Marketing research
- Database maintenance
- Follow-up campaigns

You can calculate roughly that for each long-distance customer who calls when you do not have a toll-free 800, 888, or 877 number, you will gain at least two more when you do have a toll-free line. If a high percentage of those now calling long distance become customers, the average revenue per transaction may readily indicate that the cost of installing a toll-free line will be well worth it for you.

Some services charge $30 a month or less, plus per-minute use charges. Many providers offer no monthly charges, only per minute charges. Costs and services vary widely. The cost for inbound, toll-free telephone-reception and order-taking services range between $500 and $750 or more for start-up, with a monthly minimum charge of about $150 for forty orders. Additional order charges could cost anywhere from $2 and $4 or more.

ANSWERING SERVICES: YEA OR NAY?

For more than 20 years, I have been uniformly *unimpressed* by the quality and service level of the telephone answering services I've encountered. Far too many answering services rely upon semi-skilled, unenthusiastic workers who apparently have not been briefed as to the proper name of the company for which they are answering, or the proper response to use. Many "operators" answer the phone in a hurry, quickly put callers on hold, don't listen well, don't take messages well, and frankly, my dear, couldn't give a darn about your phone call.

If you decide to use an answering service, comparative shopping is mandatory. Some answering services enable you to leave messages for specific callers. Others can answer questions about your business. Depending on the type of service you desire and how much you're willing to pay, some companies can engage in order taking.

Specifically, for home-based service providers, the marginal value of employing an answering service in support of your marketing efforts is unclear. Since telephone answering machines and various call-forwarding options cover a fairly wide latitude, the advantages of using an answering service may be entirely subjective. Here are some guidelines for retaining an answering service to handle your calls:

1. Get recommendations from friends or associates in business who retain answering services. The next time you call someone who uses an answering service whose service impresses you, ask for the name and phone number of the manager or owner of the answering service.
2. Call three to five answering services and discuss the range of services, costs, employee qualifications, other types of businesses served, and length of time in business. Ask for names of referrals or letters of praise or commendation.
3. If you attempt a trial run with an answering service, do so for the shortest time possible. Five to 7 days will give you a reasonable idea of how your calls get handled.
4. Once the service is in place, call your own office throughout the day, posing different questions and leaving different messages. Also have your spouse, children, or friends call the service so that you gain a full measure of its effectiveness.

Like it or not, the service you employ will represent the first (and regrettably, perhaps, only) impression that first-time callers have of your business and your services or products. Never retain a marginally effective answering service.

Here is a summary of the marketing advantages and disadvantages of employing an answering service:

Advantages
- Offers a live person answering the call of another person
- Can potentially be more helpful than a fixed message
- Can write up orders or perform other services for a fee
- Can be retained for specified hours, such as peak times

Disadvantages
- Can convey a poor first impression
- Can get names and numbers wrong
- Costly, particularly compared to answering machines
- May not pick up within four rings
- May frequently put callers on hold

WHEN YOUR BUSINESS RELOCATES OR YOUR PHONE NUMBER CHANGES

If you relocate outside of a local area or if your phone number changes, take immediate steps to ensure that no phone calls or messages to you are lost. If your phone number is changed, the telephone company will offer, free of charge, a recording that provides callers with the new number. There is no set time for which the phone company will offer this service, although you can count on about one year.

By far, the worst message callers can receive if you have moved or changed your number, in terms of home-based marketing, is one announcing that your number has been disconnected. *Most callers will conclude that you are out of business and will make no further effort to find you.* Yikes!

One way to avoid this is to retain the original phone number, pay the minimum monthly fee, and direct the phone company to present a prerecorded message that directs callers to your new phone number. In the short run, you could even install your own answering machine and accomplish the same end. Upon request, and/or for a only nominal monthly fee that you pay, some phone companies will allow callers to receive your new number for years after you've relocated.

After you move, periodically call your old number to keep tabs on what message callers are receiving. If your number has been reassigned to someone else, make arrangements with your successor, paying if necessary, to have your calls forwarded to your new number. Particularly if you have to abandon a dedicated business line, every call is important. You have spent considerable time and effort building your home-based business, and missed calls represent missed revenue.

Any time you move or change phone numbers, personally call or write to all of your key customers or clients, informing them of the changes. Then, for the next 4 to 6 months, continue to send reminder notes with all business correspondence. Every 12 months, 20% of the population moves or changes phone numbers. The people you sell to cannot be expected to automatically update your address or phone number after one written notice.

DON YOUR TELEPHONE HEADSET

Among the key items missing from the equipment purchases of home-based entrepreneurs is one of the least expensive and most effective devices for marketing purposes—the telephone headset. If you spend as little as 30 minutes daily on the phone, the headset will help you to make those minutes among the most productive portions of the day.

As with many types of equipment in our multi-technical society, headsets come with a variety of options. These include quality of headgear, size and softness of ear pieces, sound, clarity, volume control, and portability.

If you have never experienced the overwhelming advantage of using a headset to both field and make telephone calls, an enjoyable experience awaits you. Independent of the level of your skills, the use of a headset will automatically increase them.

Here are the advantages and disadvantage of using a telephone headset to support your telemarketing efforts:

Advantages
- Inexpensive
- Two-minute learning period
- Ability to stay on the phone, fatigue-free

- Hands-free capability, enabling you to do other things, e.g., file, take notes, and move items around while on the phone
- Undetectable to the other party
- Lightweight and modular for portability
- Extension cords available for increased mobility
- Cordless models available
- Volume control

Disadvantages
- Looks funny (not a true disadvantage!)
- More potential clutter for your desk

HOT TIPS/INSIGHTS FROM CHAPTER 5

- When answering your own phone, speak slowly and clearly so that each syllable in your company name is distinguishable. A rushed greeting or expression of your company's name can signal to callers that you rush your work.
- Treat every call as if it is from a major client or customer.
- Answer with a smile, and use the caller's name.
- Ask questions. They indicate your interest in the caller.
- If considering an answering service, do heavy comparison shopping, then frequently monitor the firm you select.
- To develop an effective Yellow Pages advertisement, think from the reader's point of view, keep the ad clean and simple, and distinguish your business from the competition. Are your years in business important to customers?
- Install a toll-free number if a significant portion of your revenue is derived from clients or customers outside your local calling area.
- Buy and use a telephone headset even if you speak on the phone only 30 minutes daily.

CHAPTER 6

Dialing for
Dollars

*Even with the enormous impact of the Internet, don't
underestimate the power of a well-timed, persuasive
phone call. Every day home-based entrepreneurs
attract lucrative clients and generate large volume
sales simply by getting on the phone.*

Answering the calls that come is one thing; using the phone
to prospect for new business can be a make-or-break activity for the long-term viability of your home-based business.
With one telephone line, an effective strategy for telemarketing is to reserve some part of the week, preferably a Tuesday,
Wednesday, or Thursday morning, and mow down eight to ten calls
at a sitting, using your telephone headset and two-way recording
device. Since you will be tying up your only line, and since
prospects who are not in when you call and wish to get back to you
may not be able to get through, tell all parties that you will be available for return calls during the afternoon of that same day, preferably between 1:30 and 3:30.

If you're equipped with two telephone lines, and this makes
more sense with every passing day, an effective strategy is to make
all of your calls on the non-business line (if this is not disruptive to
others in your household) while keeping your business telephone

line open. If a call comes in on the business line while you are already on another line, you have the option of answering it (generally not recommended, though sometimes practical) or having your answering machine or answering service field the call.

TELEPHONE SCRIPTS

To determine the underlying principles that cause us to say "yes" when confronted with an effective presentation, in person or on the phone, Arizona State University psychologist Robert Cialdini attended several sales training sessions. He found that the avalanche of choices confronting individuals today, combined with the information overload they experience in their daily lives, has forced many people to take short cuts to decision making.

In his book, *Influence: The Psychology of Modern Persuasion*, Cialdini says that "we respond to trigger features such as friendship, commitment, consensus, authority, and obligation." These trigger features "tell us almost automatically when we can correctly say 'yes' to a request." Cialdini found that the most effective sales people and sales training today incorporate such trigger features into their sales presentations.

One way to ensure that your outbound marketing efforts will be fruitful is to use a script. A well developed script can incorporate the trigger features that prompt targets to be more responsive. Indeed, telemarketing veterans, whether from commercial or home-based offices, know that using a well written or well rehearsed script is the most effective procedure for generating new business. To be an effective prospector is to be effective on the telephone. There is no getting around it.

Unfortunately, you may be among the legions of HBEs who are even reticent to use the phone. If so, it may be helpful to recognize that the phone is simply a tool. Like other tools that you use such as a computer, modem, copier, or fax machine, it requires following certain procedures.

Most important in using the telephone for marketing purposes is to relax. Your calls need to convey a professional, even-paced, upbeat message. Never make calls when you are tired, have just received bad news, are time-pressed, or otherwise preoccupied.

As I mentioned in the previous chapter, being on the phone is a full-time activity in itself. Staring out the window, toying with items on your desk, or otherwise dividing your attention generally will diminish your capacity to market your services. Find a phone system in which you can be comfortable and organized. Then ensure that your phone is positioned properly on your desk or other flat surface.

PROSPECT DATA SHEET

Date: __/__/__, __/__/__, __/__/__, __/__/__

      1   2   3   4

Name of contact: _____

Organization: _____

Telephone number: _____

Fax: _____ E-mail: _____

Results of contact(s): _____

_____

_____

_____

_____

Frequently, annual issues of key professional, trade, or industrial magazines or newsletters contain directories of members, rosters of companies that will be exhibiting at trade shows, or other valuable lists that you can use in your telemarketing efforts.

Once you have identified some of the key publications read by the market you wish to serve, you can write to those publications and determine if they sell or rent their subscriber mailing lists. You may also be able to exchange prospect lists with other professionals with whom you do not compete, who serve the same market that you do.

How to Retain the Data

There are many ways that you can quickly and easily organize your prospecting activities. One is to simply design a prospecting form to capture valuable information (elementary sample on page 95) for your overall efforts. This form could be designed using your PC, purchased at an office supply store, or prepared manually.

As you begin to accumulate information the forms could be maintained on a disk, in a card file, or a in three-ring notebook. Even in the computer age, a hard copy notebook may still work best depending on what you offer and how you work. The manner in which you retain this information is up to you—what best supports your operating style and what you're trying to accomplish.

All prospecting data, even from prospects that you have no chance of ever converting into a customer, may represent valuable information that supports your overall marketing effort; i.e., you learn things that strengthen your understanding of your prospective customers in general.

The Natural Speaking You

The key to an effective script is being natural, unhurried, and quietly confident. When you greet people in person you don't usually say, "Good morning, my name is Joe Smith. How are you this morning?" This is outdated language and will likely receive unenthusiastic responses. *Launch right into why you're calling.*

"Mr. Jones, I am Joe Smith of Joe Smith Consulting. I'm calling because I've found that firms in your field are currently experiencing XYZ problems, and we have been effective in handling such problems."

Even if your call intrudes on the other party, who wouldn't be interested in hearing a little more following that opening? If you're anxious about calling or unsure of your technique, your insecurity will be transmitted to the other party. As a result, you probably won't generate new business.

Many otherwise successful business people approach telemarketing with fear and trepidation. An easy way to get over your concerns about calling is to envision how some of your best customers feel about the services or products you provide. If you're starting in business, envision how customers or clients will feel once you have had the opportunity to serve them.

Consider this: If you're effective speaking to friends or your spouse, then why wouldn't you be effective in influencing prospective clients over the phone? There isn't that much difference! Think about the people who call you out of the blue. If they're upbeat, direct, poised, and professional, you tend to give them the courtesy of a couple of minutes of your time, regardless of what they're offering.

Hereafter, whenever you catch yourself listening to an effective telemarketer, time yourself—you'll find that you are often devoting 5, 8, or 10 minutes to such calls. Now recall the last time you received a call from someone who sounded unsure of himself, ill at ease, or apologetic. You sought to get off the phone as quickly as possible, saying "Sorry, not interested." You departed from the conversation without thinking twice.

PREPARING YOUR ENVIRONMENT FOR EFFECTIVE TELEMARKETING

Before you pick up the phone, consider the best times to call.
The table below will help you get started.

WHEN TO CALL

Prospects	Best Time to Call
Accountants	Daily, but not between April 16th and January 4th
Bankers	Before 10 a.m. or after 3 p.m.
Builders and contractors	Before 9 a.m. or after 5 p.m.
Clergy	Monday and Tuesday
Dentists	Before 9:30 a.m.
Doctors (including surgeons)	Between 9 and 11 a.m.; after 4 p.m.
Grocers	Between 1 and 3 p.m.
Engineers	Between 4 and 5 p.m.
Executives and top managers	Between 7 and 8:30 a.m.; after 10:30 a.m.
Home-based entrepreneurs	Starting at 7:30 a.m.; after 5:30 p.m.
Lawyers	Between 11 a.m. and 2 p.m.
Goverent employees	Call at home after 6 p.m.
Merchants, store managers, and department heads	After 10:30 a.m.
Pharmacists	Between 1 and 3 p.m.
Professors and teachers	At home, between 6 and 7 p.m.
Publishers and printers	After 3 p.m.
Secretaries, clerical workers	Call at home after 6 p.m.
Stockbrokers	Before 10 a.m. or after 3 p.m.
Trainers, consultants	Any time
Web designers and PC gurus	Between 2 p.m. and 11 p.m.

As you gain more experience calling preferred targets, you will gain an increasing sense of the best times to call and not to call. Make sure that you will not be interrupted during your telemarketing campaign. If you have to, hang a "Do Not Disturb" sign outside your door.

Next arrange your desk to support your telemarketing efforts: in other words, clear away everything not used for this campaign. Items to place before you include: the list of names and phone numbers you intend to call, an appointment calendar or scheduling software, a pen and pad to take plenty of notes, or as discussed earlier, prospect data sheets such as the one shown below:

It is unwise to click away on your PC or laptop while calling prospects. They can hear the clicking sound, and it distracts them from the overall conversation. (Clickless keyboards are available, but they're not perfect, some clicking can still be heard.)

Take short rests periodically. Stand up and stretch. When using a telephone headset, move around your desk. Shortly thereafter, get back to calling. Even if you run into five clunkers in a row, the next call could be a long-term, high-paying client.

USING A TELEPHONE HEADSET, TWO-WAY RECORDING, A PC, AND A FAX

For 6 years, Aaron worked in one of the world's top forty executive recruiting firms, headquartered in New York City. At the age of 36, he decided to make his move, relocating à la Diane Keaton in the 1980s movie *Baby Boom*, to upstate Vermont. He did not abandon the executive recruitment business, however. Armed with a couple of major accounts he was able to line up during his last year in New York, Aaron set up shop in the front corner room of a converted farm house.

Unbeknownst to people outside of the industry, executive recruitment has long been telephone-intensive. Aaron made an important investment in his home-based venture by plunking down a mere $95 for a telephone headset. The headset snapped into his existing telephone line immediately, giving him hands-free capability. While it looked a little funny, wearing the telephone headset enabled Aaron to stay on the phone for 30 and 40 minutes at a time without fatigue. Since he worked alone, he didn't care how he appeared when wearing the headset.

Aaron was often involved in long telephone calls with clients who described the type of candidate they sought and the job role the right candidate would fill. While these assignments were formally completed by contract, Aaron made sure that he got as much information as possible from the contact person by phone. His phone also had an answering machine that provided two-way recording with the push of a button.

Aaron bought several dozen audio-cassettes, 30 minutes to a side. When discussing new executive searches with his clients, he would tell them, "Wait a moment, let me get this on tape," press the two-way record button, and continue. Though every word of the conversation was captured on tape, Aaron also made extensive notes—an easy activity to undertake while wearing the telephone headset, since both hands are free.

At his discretion, he would play back the tapes, pausing frequently to make additional notes and further secure his understanding of an assignment. Once he had a clear idea of what the client was seeking, Aaron began his exhaustive search, which also involved heavy use of the telephone, Internet searches, and all other means he could think of to find prospective candidates. Sometimes he looked for the authors of well written articles as well as experts quoted in key industry publications.

He would call any contacts he had within the appropriate industry, as well as association executives, editors of industry publications, and anyone else who might be able to give him the names of qualified candidates. Aaron would frequently make ten to twelve calls in succession. Often, in less than a day, Aaron generated a list of six to eight candidates, which sometimes grew to fifteen or more on better days.

Next, it was time to contact the candidates themselves. Aaron was skilled at making calls to candidates' homes, introducing himself in such a way that they sensed that he was a professional making a legitimate search. When he encountered candidates for whom he thought there was significant potential, he would invite them to mail, fax, or e-mail a resume. After reviewing the resume and speaking with the candidate at least one other time, he would schedule a flight to visit the candidate personally.

The candidates he placed were in the six-figure income range. When Aaron made a successful placement, he grossed $35,000 or more. Not being one to make unnecessary trips, Aaron traveled only when he felt sure that the candidate had a high potential of filling the job in question.

One of Aaron's rules of travel was never to make a trip for a single purpose. If he visited a client or a job candidate, he always lined up several other appointments either in that same city, at airport stopovers, or on small side trips. Because his telephone headset was modular, he brought it on road trips and often continued his calling schedule from hotel rooms.

To record conversations while on the road, Aaron purchased a telephone coupler and an adapter plug that fits into a standard cassette recorder and attaches by a suction cup to the receiver of a telephone at the other end. This simple device, retailing for under $3, enabled Aaron to tape phone conversations (although the transmission quality was not as good as that of his two-way recorder at home).

As a standard practice, Aaron kept in contact with clients and candidates via e-mail, fax, and phone. Some currently unsuccessful candidates could serve as bird dogs (scouts) for future search campaigns and might be the appropriate candidates themselves for other positions.

Aaron bought a scanner and read resumes he received onto a master file on disk. Using file-search software, he was able to find a particular candidate, and arrange the resumes based on any word reference, attribute, or character string. All the while Aaron continued to use telephone skills to scout for new clients. He was familiar with the needs of firms in a couple of key industries, and knew how to identify and make contact with such firms.

Aaron considered converting from telephone headset to speaker phone, but he found that the speaker phone made many people uncomfortable. The voice quality even of top-of-the-line models still did not match mouth-to-receiver systems. Speaker phone also created problems for his two-way telephone conversation recording system.

Later, he found a telephone headset lighter than his first, a model with an extension-free option that enabled him to walk around his office freely, retrieve hard-copy files, or handle a variety of other activities while on hold.

In the midst of searches, as Aaron spoke to more and more candidates, he would frequently replay initial conversations with the client to regain a precise understanding of the type of person being sought. This kept him highly focused on the client's needs rather than on his memory of the client's needs.

In a few years, Aaron was grossing nearly $285,000 a year while living in a healthier, less stressful environment. His third year in business he got married; two years thereafter he and his wife had their first child. He renovated the attic and moved his office there. Today, Aaron earns strong revenues and has time for his family and the great outdoors.

CONFRONTING THE GATEKEEPERS

Anyone who has ever telemarketed has encountered plenty of receptionists and others hired to shield the party to whom he is trying to speak. The higher your target in the organization (and the larger the organization), the more complex the screening process will be. The best strategy for handling a third party who stands between you and your target contact is to level with the person.

"May I ask what this is in reference to?" (Pleasantly): "I sent her a package last week and promised to call her at this time. Is she in the office?"

Ask the intermediary to suggest the best time for you to call back. If given a time, thank the intermediary and convey the message to the target that you will be calling back at X o'clock. Then, of course, do so.

If the intermediary can't suggest a time to call back, then offer one. If you're calling in the morning, choose a time during the afternoon. If you are calling in the afternoon, choose a time the next morning. Even if the intended party is not in, the fact that you called when you said you would and properly left a message will score you some points. The probability of the target calling back increases when he is handed a message indicating you called exactly when you said you would.

If the intermediary is uncooperative, remain pleasant but professional. You may encounter a stone wall: "He is extremely busy right now and won't be available for several days. Why don't you leave your number, and I will see that he gets it." If you are confronted with this type of response or one that is even less informative, you have several options.

First, if you can, state your business using such words as "I have a message of importance," and continue by issuing a polite order: "Kindly put me through to him." Or you can inform the intermediary that you will be calling back Tuesday at X o'clock.

Alternatively, you might inform the intermediary that you will send a follow-up letter or fax that in essence says, "When I called you last week, I learned it was a busy period for you. I will give you a call next Wednesday at 11:30."

Don't make the gatekeeper defensive

Whatever you do, don't suggest that the intermediary is wrong. Intermediaries are paid to do what they do, and may frequently be confronted by overly aggressive, rude, or otherwise unprofessional callers. Stand your ground, remain unflustered and professional, and convey your intentions. Your professional demeanor does get back to the target person and will pay off in the long run.

One executive observed that he can tell by the way callers treat his receptionist whether or not he'll want to get in touch with them. Callers who are respectful with targets but rough with receptionists, he feels, are revealing their true nature.

Confronting Voice Mail Options

It is so easy for people to screen calls (and outright ignore them) because of voice mail options, that one could devote a whole book to the topic. However, I can boil down to a couple paragraphs the essence of everything it takes to be an effective home-based telemarketer when confronting voice mail.

Use the same approaches, techniques, and courtesies when leaving someone a voice mail or answering machine message that you would when reaching them live on the first try. Never leave a message that you later will regret leaving.

Some telemarketing gurus suggest not leaving a message in many instances, particularly if you have other options for reaching the party or if you're making a follow-up call. Why? Your call is easy to ignore. Conversely, many experts recommend rehearsing opening call and follow-up call dialogues so that if you do confront voice mail and feel it best to leave a message, you'll be offering your best.

YOU CAN MAKE THE PHONE WORK FOR YOU

If you are among the millions of home-based telephone marketers who are fearful (or at least a little gun-shy) of using the phone to generate new business, take heart. Like learning to drive a car or operating a computer for the first time, your skill and effectiveness is best judged after you've spent a couple of hours in training.

Having arrived at that point in life where you've chosen to earn your income at home, you probably already possess the ability to influence others in conversation and over the phone. With a little practice and the adoption of a few basic techniques, you'll do fine as a home-based telemarketer.

HOT TIPS/INSIGHTS FROM CHAPTER 6

- If you telemarket, use a script!
- Get a second phone line before going to Chapter 7.
- The key to using a script effectively is being natural, unhurried, and quietly confident.
- To double your productivity, use a telephone headset when you make or field telephone calls.
- Rehearse a succinct, compelling 20- or 30-second message that you'll give in the event you encounter voice mail or an answering machine.
- If you're effective in face-to-face discussions, you can be persuasive over the phone.

CHAPTER 7

E-mailing, Faxing, and Mailing from Home

Before e-mail and fax messages can truly be effective, generally you have to establish a working relationship with a prospect. Otherwise, whatever you send will have a hard time standing out from the mass of messages your targets are already receiving.

It's unlikely that e-mail or faxes in and of themselves will win you any new business. Before you can be effective with them, you'll need to have to have "broken through" to a prospect. Perhaps your printed literature is outstanding. Or, you may have a captivating Web site. Or you're a marketing whirlwind on the phone.

The hard, cold reality of e-mail is that in less than half a decade, it's gone from moderate use to overuse to abuse. In a full decade, among those having *business relationships* with one another, faxes have gone from novelty to convenience to staple and, among those *prospecting to others*, from to novelty to mass marketing vehicle to a stringently regulated medium.

While it is a bit more difficult to control the crushing effects of mass e-mail (spam), all but those who disseminate it are eager to see it squelched. Even if spam did not exist, e-mail, in and of itself, would not be an effective stand-alone or entire marketing vehicle because it is too easily:

- Ignored
- Misread
- Deleted

Nevertheless, creative options abound for sending messages and information at a reasonable cost that help you win or retain customers. This chapter looks at ways to ensure that your home-based marketing transmission has the best chance of having the desired impact. Let's start with fax capabilities, easing into the use of e-mail as a supporting or alternative technology.

FAXES—EFFECTIVENESS AMPLIFIED BY ONE'S CREATIVITY

Some home-based marketers use fax transmissions to announce price revisions to regular and prospective customers, or as a "keep in touch" vehicle to build upon an earlier message. Certainly following a phone call or in-person marketing presentation, a fax transmission that outlines key points previously made is an appropriate and efficient form of follow-up.

The Beauty of Fax before 8 a.m.

Depending on the type of service you retain, long-distance phone and fax rates may be lower after 5 p.m. and before 8 a.m. Many commercial offices and home-based entrepreneurs have dedicated fax lines, or fax lines than share limited online time. Since in many offices a gatekeeper (receptionist) or office early birds often arrive before 8 a.m., you can inexpensively submit a fax message to be forwarded to your target. The same holds true even if the office is closed.

Each morning, Arlene, a design consultant, assembles a stack of fax messages for long-distance transmission between 7:30 and 7:55 a.m. By reserving this time for fax transmissions, she is able to cut her long distance bill and make a notable marketing impact. Her messages and information are among the first items encountered by the recipients that day.

Using the Fax as a Substitute for the Phone

Suppose you've been away from your desk all day. You check your voice mail or answering machine, and there are six messages. Many calls can be answered more quickly and effectively by a fax message. If you live on the East Coast, the West Coast caller who simply needs a yes-or-no answer can be reached inexpensively after 5 p.m. your time, while it's still mid-afternoon West Coast time.

Instead of spelling out a five-line message to a distracted receptionist, or having to slowly and carefully speak to a voice mail system, simply fax back the original fax you received along with your quick hand-written reply. All the identifying information is already included.

Suppose you're trying to reach someone by phone and, despite using automatic redial, you're having trouble. Send a quick message by fax saying "Having trouble reaching you by phone," or "Will be available between _____ and _____." Such a transmission accomplishes several objectives. You get your message through to the party you have been trying to reach, your phone line remains open to make or receive other calls, and the option is always available to include additional information on your fax transmission.

Contract Negotiations by Fax

The fax machine can speed up the time in which a contract is negotiated and completed. Since stalls and delays are often used as tactics (never by you, always by the other guy!), an extra bit of preparation and organization is necessary from your end to conduct an advantageous contract negotiation. Here are the essentials you will need to make it work:

- Make several copies of the contract. If you have to mark or resubmit pages, you will be ready to do so without delay.
- Many negotiators find it useful to make three columns on a page headed, "Must have," "Would like to have," and "Take it or leave it." Then, fill in all the contract terms that you must have, followed by those you would like to have, followed by those that you could take or leave. These three lists give you a visual summary of how you are progressing during the negotiation.

- Use a telephone headset so that you can stretch or move about during phone conversations, particularly if the conversation goes for longer than 15 minutes.
- Keep an extra pad and paper close by, along with any notes of key points you want to make during the negotiation.
- Post any reminders to yourself about not giving in, standing firm, when to come on strong, when to lay back, etc., so that your telephone performance is at its best.
- Keep a mirror nearby (a blank monitor screen can work as well) to note your expression as you speak. For the most part, smile and stay upbeat and enthusiastic, though for effect you may choose to exhibit other emotions.

If negotiations aren't completed as swiftly as you wanted, by using fax transmissions and the system described above, you will still cut precious days off turnaround times and, hopefully, close on contracts sooner. (You can offer instant revisions and new terms via fax machine.)

Here is a quick summary of the advantages and disadvantages of conducting negotiations with the aid of the fax machine:

Advantages
- Speeds up negotiations
- Reduces wasted time both parties spend trying to catch each other
- If used systematically, ensures that your "must have" and "would like to have" items will be addressed
- Demonstrates your efficiency and professionalism

Disadvantages
- May pressure on one or both parties to complete the deal faster than is comfortable
- May lead to hasty concessions on your part

THE FAX ADVERTISEMENT-PHONE-FAX SYSTEM

Richard Connor, mentioned in Chapter 4 as a certified management consultant serving the accounting profession, devised a clever marketing system using his fax machine 5 days after buying it. To this day, I'm still amazed that so few consultants have emulated Dick's system.

One of the fundamental, continuing problems facing Dick's clients was the difficulty of writing, reviewing, and proofing proposals and submitting them to their own clients in short order. The basic dilemma for many of Dick's clients was that too much time was passing between the time they identified a new business opportunity and the time they were able to submit a high-quality proposal specifically addressing the identified need. Dick's clients wanted to close the loop to 5 to 8 days, but were presently expending 20 to 25 days.

A chief stumbling block for the accounting firms among Dick's clients was the internal review. Most firms justifiably had established procedures dictating that no proposal leaves the office before at least two partners review it. Often, partners were out of the office for days at a time. As with any document that has to be routed, corrected, and proofed, much time was consumed, way too much time to be competitive.

Dick's system consisted of first devising a simple boilerplate advertisement which, at the top, announced,

The advertisement then described Dick's background in working with hundreds of firms, his ability to write winning proposals, and the faith and confidence that so many firms placed in him.

Don't Submit That Proposal
Until You Run it by Me.

From his home-based office, Dick faxed this message to thirty-six regular clients, those with whom he *already* had a relationship.

Dick was unprepared for the response. Within 3 days, four firms took him up on his offer. Two sent proposals by express carrier the next day, since the proposals were lengthy. Dick pored over every line of both of them the same day he received them. He faxed back only the pages with changes. Two firms sent shorter proposals by fax, one of seven pages and one twelve pages long. With these shorter documents Dick phoned in the changes.

Later, a fifth firm sent its corporate capability statement, an eighteen-page document already in the production stage. Buoyed by the initial results, Dick fine-tuned his fax advertisement for submission to other familiar prospects. (He already had their fax numbers and had already been in contact previously.) The results were not as startling, but nevertheless worth the effort.

Dick found that, at a minimum, he got a call from one of every fifteen firms. Dick began preparing advertisements to appear in professional accounting publications. He also revised his advertising copy to include e-mail transmissions and, of course, express mail. Some firms are leery of sending complete proposals by modem because it provides the receiver with the proprietary proposals on disk. Also page formats and layouts, crucial for the "cosmetic" appearance of a proposal, sometimes go awry when downloaded. Nevertheless, some clients simply e-mailed their proposals.

> If you're a consultant to a profession, you can use faxes to help firms review plans, proposals, specification sheets—anything that could be improved by having a "pro" look it over and return it quickly.

By introducing this service to his key clients and then broadening his marketing efforts, Dick developed a way for accounting firms to streamline their proposal process, and enhance *their* marketing efforts. Many home-based businesses can use this system to generate additional business:

- A graphic artist sends sketches, line drawings, and mockups to clients.

- A freelance writer submits article and book proposals, finished articles, and chapters for quick consideration and review.
- A public-affairs consultant sends timely tips and messages to prospective clients, helping to convince them of the value of retaining his services.
- An attorney reviews contracts, deeds, wills, etc., with quicker turnaround time and reduced rates because she doesn't have to travel to as many meetings.
- A home-based word processor sends a faxgram to all her clients indicating that for the next few days she doesn't have enough work to do and will offer a 10% discount on all projects through Friday.
- An equipment dealer sends a message to regular buyers informing them of a bona fide great price on a limited quantity of a sought-after peripheral device.

USING DICTATION AND MAIL, OR FAX, THEN MODEM

Dave offers marketing-consulting services to businesses throughout his metro area. He's been operating out of his home office for 4 years and has perfected a system for painlessly developing proposals, sales letters, consulting reports, advertising copy, outlines, lists, and other marketing items.

When he wants to create or significantly revise a document, he first dictates his message using hand-held portable dictation equipment (readily available in the home-electronics section of major department stores).

Dave uses a microcassette recorder that holds up to sixty minutes of dictation on each side and, using a slower recording speed, can hold up to two hours on each side. He then transfers these tapes to his secretary Hana, who lives six blocks away, and runs her own home-based word-processing service.

Dave initially found Hana when he assigned a part-time worker, an eighteen-year-old student, to scan the local phone books and call word-processing services specifically to find someone who operated out of his or her home. Not surprisingly, there were several home-based secretarial services within a half-mile radius of Dave.

Dave's strategy was to obtain more individualized service at a lower price. He was not interested in using a word-processing service based in a commercial office, and he found that even with the best voice recognition dictation systems, there was still a lot work to do, that he didn't want to do. Besides, he could carry his pocket dictator with him all day long.

He transfers the microcassette tapes several ways. When Dave or one of his part-timers is headed in Hana's direction, he drops off the tapes at her home; she need not be there, since they have a pre-arranged transfer spot. When Hana is headed in Dave's direction, she picks up the tape herself. Occasionally, Dave relies on the U. S. Postal Service or couriers.

The E-mail Transmission When Hana is finished, she e-mails Dave. Hana uses her e-mail system that comes with America Online. Dave checks e-mail about three times daily, but of course, either party can phone each other at will.

After he downloads the file, using his word-processing software, Dave prints a hard copy and makes corrections, revisions, changes, and modifications directly on the hard copy. Sometimes he does this after receiving the files; sometimes it's days later. He then enters the changes himself if they are light, or assigns a student editor/helper to enter them. Dave usually reviews each file again, making any last-minute changes, and then he saves the final version.

Let's step back and observe the beauty of this system. Dave dictates his marketing materials because he does not like to type or spend long hours in front of a PC or notebook computer using voice recognition software. He feels productive simply dictating what he wants to put on paper. He is willing to pay Hana for the time to have his materials put on paper. Meanwhile, his time is free to work on other things.

When Hana transcribes the material, Dave knows from experience what relative level of quality he will get. To avoid prolonged time on the PC, Dave finds it faster and more convenient simply to print out the hard copies. Dave's total time and involvement in dictating, receiving the e-mail, printing out the hard copy, having it corrected, and saved as final is less than 30% of the time it would take him to make original entries, edit, revise, edit, proof, and print. Hence, Dave is able to devote several more hours per week to prospecting for new clients or working on projects for existing clients. He has increased his revenues significantly each year in business, while his operating expenses have increased only moderately.

Because he dictates rather than attempting to compose letters, flyers, seminar outlines, and so on, his creative juices are unleashed in ways he couldn't experience when he made original PC entries.

Often, Dave will dictate from 7:00 to 8:30 a.m before the phone starts ringing. Within 90 minutes he can dictate what used to take him a day or longer to write. Soon, Dave expects to convert to voice recognition for a least half of his dictation. As the systems become operable with palm top computers, Dave may even take it with him on the road.

How Dave's System Applies to You

If you're interested in pursuing this system, here are some parameters:

- To fill-up a 60-minute microcassette requires about 150 minutes of dictation time (because you'll make frequent pauses).
- Sixty minutes on microcassette, once transcribed, will yield about twenty-four double-spaced manuscript pages.
- Each page you dictate, therefore, requires about 6 minutes of your actual time.

You can quickly determine how long it will take for you to dictate various materials. A one-page management letter takes about 6 minutes. A twenty-page consulting report requires at least 2 hours. The longer the report or document, the greater its complexity. Thus, it may not be possible to maintain the 6-minute benchmark.

Achieving these productivity rates requires that you have a rough outline on hand when you begin dictating. You'll need notes of what you'll be dictating, as you would if you were about to enter the material on a disk. Far too many home-based marketers armed with powerful PCs and high-quality printers have never experienced the timesaving boost of dictating marketing materials—what a shame.

Why do HBEs readily invest in equipment and services that *transfer* information, but do not invest in far less expensive equipment that speeds its *development*?

One survey showed that less than one in ten home-based entrepreneurs owned dictating equipment, and only a few others had plans to purchase such equipment.

Here's a summary of the advantages and disadvantages of Dave's system for developing marketing materials using dictation equipment:

Advantages
- Stimulates creativity
- Offers substantial overall time savings
- Reduces drudgery of editing and proofing
- Enhances objectivity and focus because material is examined by two or three parties
- Uses part-time and outside help effectively
- Encourages the development of marketing support materials that otherwise might not be attempted

Disadvantages
- Time consumed in information transfers
- Unless the part-time secretary is nearby, transfer of tapes is cumbersome
- If dictation efforts are poorly organized, could create extra work

PHONE, FAX, E-MAIL, AND MAIL TO SUPPORT PROMOTION EFFORTS

Adele worked as a registered dietitian for several years before taking time out to raise three children. As her children grew up and affordable home technology become available, she began formulating the concept of her own weight- and fitness-counseling business. Adele was an aerobic fitness enthusiast, devouring books and articles on the topic and staying in excellent shape herself.

Many of her friends had relied on her sound advice for staying healthy and keeping fit. In fact, Adele's friends encouraged her to start her own weight-and-fitness counseling business. After a year of struggling to find clients and keep the business afloat, happily, business picked up sharply. Clients were making referrals on her behalf. Adele was booked at about 60% of her optimum capacity. She was able to purchase some sorely needed equipment, including a digital scale, blood-pressure monitor, and personal copier for her home-based office.

By the start of the third year, Adele was comfortable, but acknowledged that she could still be serving far more clients. In some of the magazines and newsletters Adele received, she saw articles she could easily have written. One day, after reading an article that she had found to be inadequate, she got on the phone and spoke to the editor directly, diplomatically pointing out what else the article should have said and how she might have handled it. She should have guessed that the editor would invite her, for a fee, to submit her own article.

Although untested, Adele was up to the challenge, and about a week later she had a seven-page article ready. She e-mailed it to the editor and waited for a reply. When the acceptance e-mail arrived, she noticed that both a phone and a fax number were listed at the bottom of the editor's electronic signature. The marketing flood gates opened for Adele. She called a variety of other editors, proposing other articles, asking for their fax numbers and e-mail addresses.

Over the next several months, in addition to serving existing clients and conducting her normal prospecting activities, Adele developed almost a dozen articles on various aspects of fitness, nutrition, aerobics, and diet. Her procedure for generating interest in the articles was simple but powerful. First, Adele would write the articles without discussing any of them with anyone. She knew what topics were important to her target market, she knew what she wanted to say, and she didn't want to have the pressure of conforming to someone else's guidelines.

When the articles were ready or nearly ready on disk, she called selected editors and pitched them over the phone. Sometimes, when she couldn't get the editor on the phone, she sent a one-page pitch letter by fax, which she felt would have more impact than e-mail.

Invariably, the editors called or wrote back and said yes or no to her proposed article. Eventually, nearly half of her responses were affirmative. For editors she reached by phone, Adele suggested that she could send the articles by e-mail. The editors responded affirmatively.

Adele immediately sent an article any time her discussion with an editor led her to believe that the article in question did not require any additional modifications. In those cases, Adele often got acceptances within 3 to 10 days. When an article needed some modification, or Adele sensed that the editor would not be responsive to a seemingly off-the-shelf article, she waited a day or two before sending it. Again, she got relatively quicker responses than she would have expected after mailing the article.

In 3 months, Adele had several published articles, which she had attractively reprinted in large quantities to further enhance her home-based marketing efforts. When Adele encountered a prospect, in addition to literature about her health and fitness-consulting services, she included a bylined article that greatly enhanced her overall presentation. She also selectively submitted articles by fax to some of her existing clients.

From Articles to Newspaper Coverage

One of Adele's new clients worked for the county newspaper. It wasn't a big paper, and it certainly didn't compete with the morning city paper. However, it had a circulation of 46,500 and was respected within the community. Adele's reporter client was interested in doing a small feature on Adele's services, an idea to which Adele obviously was responsive.

A few weeks after the article appeared in the county paper, Adele got several calls. About five callers became clients. The whole chain of events was lucky, and Adele knew it. She wondered though if it was possible to *systemize* one's media coverage. Like many business executives and entrepreneurs, she had already tried submitting press releases but found the acceptance ratio to be disappointingly low. Using her persuasive telephone skills, her fax machine, mail, and e-mail, however, she was able to devise a system that increased the rate at which she was able to obtain some press coverage. Here's what Adele did:

Using a part-time helper (Chapter 11), she tracked which reporters at which publications covered topics related to health, diet, and fitness. At Adele's instructions, the part-timer began clipping articles written by these reporters. Once a month, Adele would review the file of each reporter and then call each. Over the phone she would praise him for some previous article and then discuss:

- Some new twist, theme, or variation that she had discovered
- How she applied this in her practice
- How this discovery had benefited her clients

If the conversation got rolling, then and there she would suggest that she could fax or e-mail some information, not more than a few pages worth, immediately. Invariably, the reporter would say yes; Adele would thank him and then feed a few pages into the fax machine or send an e-mail, depending on what material she had in mind to transmit; i.e., an attractive article reprint could only be faxed, whereas original material on disk could be e-mailed.

Knowing that fax transmissions are not high-quality reprints, Adele sometimes would also send a hard-copy backup by mail with a stick-em note thanking the reporter for his interest. Overall, this system, as with any other dealing with the media, is not foolproof. Often, reporters do not follow up on the information, and no coverage results.

To a far greater extent than she had experienced when disseminating press releases, however, Adele was getting coverage. Her PR goal was to get some mention in at least one publication per month, and after a number of months she was able to achieve this.

About 18 months after she developed this system, business was booming. She even considered renting commercial space and maintaining only an administrative home office. Adele requested that each new client complete a form concerning his or her medical history. At the bottom of the form, Adele always asked where the client had learned about her services. More and more were referring to articles they saw about her; Adele's PR system was paying off. She was now appearing in more than one local publication each month.

What's more, reporters to whom she had spoken but who had not done a feature on her nevertheless kept her information on file. In the course of their business, as they covered other topics involving health, diet, fitness, and so forth, eventually they either referred to what Adele had sent them or called her directly for quotes. Of course, anyone seeking updated information received it immediately via Adele's fax or e-mail.

SOME E-MAIL MARKETING GROUND RULES

With the advent of commercial online services such as CompuServe and AOL, and Internet software such as Netscape and Eudora, use of e-mail has proliferated to the point where many people log on only to find dozens, if not hundreds, of e-mail messages per day. Use of e-mail has gone from use to overuse to abuse in record time. I do not recommend using e-mail as a marketing tool until you have made prior contact in person, by phone, or by mail. Otherwise, it's simply too easy to have your message bleeped into the far reaches of cyberspace, never to be seen or thought of again.

When using e-mail to enhance other aspects of your marketing efforts, try not to offer "bozo" messages (see below) or those that might be perceived as such. Never use symbols such as ******** ======= +++++++ or the like as borders. Don't over-promise anything, especially in the header and on the first line of the message. Using the words "Money," "Income," "Earn," "Sex," "Free," "Breakthrough," and "Hot" among others will get you bleeped by most recipients.

It may also pay for you to get a private e-mail address, one that you dispense with great reserve so as to maintain a bastion in which you can receive a few high-quality messages.

What kind of messages do you send? Those that are short, get right to the point, fully identify yourself, and present an active return address. Draw upon all the techniques discussed in the book. If you can't be convincing in a letter, brochure, or flyer, realistically, you have even less of a chance in an e-mail. Nevertheless, depending on to whom you are appealing and why, e-mail can be quite convenient.

SUPPORT YOUR LOCAL POSTAL WORKER— MAILING OPTIONS

As you've seen, mailing techniques to support home-based marketing are presented in cases and anecdotes in this chapter and throughout the book. Mailing options available through private, commercial express-mail services such as Fedex, DHL, Roadway, Airborne, and Purolator Courier, and through parcel service such as UPS and Roadway, are well known to most entrepreneurs.

From a marketing standpoint, *overuse* of express mail has had diminishing impact on recipients. Use it when you have to, but forget about it as a substantial aid to marketing. It makes more sense in many times, and can generate receiver impact, to use the U. S. Postal System's other options—for all its troubles—if you know how to use it effectively.

E-Mail Filters to Keep *You* Sane

Guy Kawasaki, author of *How to Drive Your Competition Crazy*, says to set up some "bozo filters." You can safely ignore, for example, any message that:

- Contains a suspicious e-mail address
- Is cc'd to more than four other parties
- Appears in all capital letters
- Is prefaced with "FYI," "for immediate release," or "first, some background"
- Is longer than five paragraphs. (The action is in the first and last paragraph.)

Standard Mailing Options 101

Here's a mercifully brief description from the public information office of the U. S. Postal Service of some standard services, followed by descriptions of services to safeguard, protect, and document your packages.

- Express mail service is the Post Office's fastest service and is comparable to commercial services. Express Mail Next Day Service provides several options for both private and business customers who require overnight delivery of letters and packages. To use this service, take your shipment to any designated Express Mail post office, generally by 5 p.m., or deposit it in an Express Mail collection box. Your mailing will be delivered by 12 p.m. the next day (weekends and holidays included) to "most" cities. Also, you may be able to arrange for pick-up at your location. Call your local Post Office to see if this option is available for you.

  There are more than 26,000 post offices and more than 10,000 special Express Mail collection boxes in which you can deposit your parcels. Your letter carrier can accept pre-paid Express Mail shipments at the time your mail is delivered. The Post Office will supply you with mailing containers (envelopes, boxes, and tubes) and the necessary mailing labels free of charge.

- Priority mail is first-class mail (weighing up to 70 pounds), and measuring up to 108 inches in combined length and girth. Based on availability, the Post Office provides free Priority Mail labels and stickers. Insurance (see below) can be purchased on Priority Mail.

  Watch out! Although advertised as "2–3 day delivery," from my experience and those of several other entrepreneurs, delivery ranges from 2 to 8 days. Packages currently are not tracked, but are hardly ever lost. The red, white, and blue packages do have marketing impact, if for no other reason than most people don't receive that much priority mail within a given month.

- First-class mail is designed for letters, postcards, greeting cards, personal notes, and checks and money orders in packages weighing 16 ounces or less. You cannot insure ordinary first-class mail. However, additional services such as certificate of mailing, certified, return receipt, and restricted delivery can be purchased at the option of the mailer. If your first-class mail is not letter size, make sure it is marked "First Class," or use a green-bordered large envelope. First class mail is actually USPS's forte; they are designed to move this category of mailing most efficiently. A new generation of scanners can even read hand addressed envelopes. Bar coding makes first class mail even faster. Chances are your word-processing system already contains a simple bar coding procedure.
- Third-class mail, also referred to as bulk business or advertising mail, may be sent by anyone, but is used most often by large mailers. This class includes printed material and merchandise weighing less than 16 ounces. There are two rate structures for this class: single piece and bulk rate. Individuals may use this class of mail for mailing light-weight parcels, and insurance can be purchased to cover loss or damage of articles.
- Forwarding mail: When you move, fill out a Change of Address card in advance at your local post office. When possible, notify your post office at least one month before your move. First-class mail is forwarded at no charge. Magazines, newspapers, and other second-class mail are forwarded at no charge for 60 days from the effective date of a change-of-address order. Your post office has information about holding mail, temporary changes of address, and forwarding and return of other classes of mail.

Postal Protection and Documentation

- Certified mail provides a receipt of mailing, and a record of delivery is maintained at the recipient's post office. You can also pay an additional fee for a receipt to indicate proof of delivery. For valuables and irreplaceable items, the Postal Service recommends using insured or registered mail.

- Collect on delivery (COD) is useful when you want to collect for merchandise (up to a maximum value) as it is delivered. COD service may be used for merchandise sent by first-class, third-class, or fourth-class mail. The merchandise must have been ordered by the addressee. The Postal Service includes in its fee insurance protection against loss or damage. COD items may also be sent as registered mail.

- Insurance can be purchased up to $5,000 for standard mail, a certain maximum on registered mail, and a far lesser maximum for third and fourth-class mail. Insurance can also be purchased for merchandise mailed at the priority mail or first-class mail rates. With articles insured for more than a threshold amount, a receipt of delivery is signed by the recipient and filed at the delivering post office. The amount of insurance coverage for loss is the actual value, less any depreciation. Sorry, no payments are made for sentimental losses or for any expenses incurred as a result of the loss.

- Registered mail: The Postal Service regards this as its most secure mailing option. It is designed to provide added protection for valuable and important mail. Postal insurance may be purchased, at the option of the mailer, for articles valued at more than $100 up to a maximum of $25,000. Return-receipt and restricted-delivery services are available for an additional fee. Registered articles are controlled from the point of mailing to delivery. First-class postage is required on registered mail.

- Restricted delivery: Except for Express Mail service, you can request restricted delivery when purchasing return-receipt service. Restricted delivery means that delivery is made only to the addressee or to someone who is authorized in writing to receive mail for the addressee. Such mail when addressed to officials of government agencies, members of the legislative and judicial branches of federal and state governments, members of the diplomatic corps, minors, and individuals under guardianship, however, can be delivered to an agent without written authorization from the addressee.

- Return receipt is your proof of delivery and is available on mail that you send by COD or Express Mail, which is insured for more than $25 or that you register or certify. The return receipt shows who signed for the item and the date it was delivered. For an additional fee, you can get an exact address of delivery or request restricted-delivery service.

- Special delivery service can be bought on all classes of mail except bulk third class. It provides for delivery, even on Sundays and holidays, during hours that extend beyond the hours for delivery of ordinary mail. This service is available to all customers served by city carriers and to other customers within a one-mile radius of the delivery post office. Note that special delivery may be handled by your regular carrier if it's available before the carrier departs for morning deliveries. Call your Post Office about the availability of special-delivery service.

- International mail: You can send air and surface mail to virtually all foreign countries. There are many types of international mail, such as:

> Letters and Cards—includes letters, letter packages, lightweight aerogrammes, and postcards
> Other Articles—includes printed matter, matter for the blind, and small packets
> Parcel Post
> Global Priority mail

With Global Priority Mail, registry service with limited reimbursement protection is available for letters and cards and other articles to many countries, and insurance is available for parcel post to most countries.

The next time you're in the Post Office ask for the *Guide to Postal Rates and Fees*, which elaborates on these mailing options.

Mailing Enhancements and Added Touches

With any type of package you send, there are inexpensive ways to make it stand out and hence aid your overall marketing effort.

Using Quick Stampers

I use quick-stamped messages, available through any stationery store or quick-copy center, for marketing purposes. One stamp reads:

> *Here is the information that you requested!*

I stamp this on the outside of the envelope any time I send information to another person following his letter, fax, e-mail, or telephone request for it. In our society, in which the typical person is subjected to a 60-foot stack of paper every year, even those who ask for your information are prone to forget that they initiated the request. The simple message above, stamped on the outside of the envelope, someplace above the address, reminds the addressee of his request. Often, I circle the stamped message with a red or green felt-tip marker for emphasis.

The same such message could also be generated with your computer using label paper. If you have color printer, all the better.

Here's another enhancement. I often stamp the following message on the outside lower left-hand corner of a self-addressed stamped envelope that I include with mailings:

> *Please send your business card. Thank you!*

Many people are responsive to this request for their business card, particularly because there is little effort involved. I keep a notebook of business cards, often in addition to entering the names onto a database software program. I insert them into plastic windows on a sheet that holds ten cards per side, twenty cards in all. Information about a prospect on disk is not quite the same as having a business card. The card holds clues as to the nature of his business and job. Having another party mail his business card to you helps increase the probability of future connections.

Dale Carnegie once said that if you want to make friends with someone, ask him "to do a favor for you." I would add, keep the request small and something he can readily accomplish. Asking someone to send you his business card is a small request that can readily be accomplished.

Another stamper that I use simply reads:

> *Please be sure that we have your current e-mail address and, if applicable, Web site information.*

People are happy to make sure that you have their correct e-mail address. To think that one is not receiving one's e-mail messages (the non-spam variety) can be disconcerting!

Using a Speed Reply System

Hal uses his copier to create what he calls "speed replies" in support of his overall marketing efforts. Whenever he receives a letter from someone, particularly someone he already knows, he simply writes his reply on the bottom of the other party's letter, copies it, stamps it "speed reply", and mails or faxes it back immediately. Although a variety of duplicate letter forms are available, Hal finds it more effective to simply run his replies through his copier.

On occasion, he uses the reverse side to write or print a longer, more detailed reply. He finds this simple system to be particularly effective with people who are interested in a quick response and who are not protocol oriented.

Using Tailored Cassette Letters for Marketing

Carefully tailored, 3-minute cassette tapes can be used in another creative and inexpensive marketing strategy. Find a local cassette-tape distributor who offers 2-, 3-, or 4-minute cassettes, or cassette tapes of any length you need. Then record your own custom message to selected targets. When your recipient first receives the tape, he'll see by the size of the tape spool that the message is short.

Many recipients will actually play your cassette message within a day or two after receiving it, particularly if they commute to work (aren't you glad you work at home?) Let's face it: Most people don't often receive 3-minute cassettes in the mail. Depending on what you're offering, and to whom, your message will stand out from the daily stack of printed materials that busy individuals receive.

When you prepare your own recorded, custom message, you have many options. You can speaking slowly and clearly in an authoritative voice, or coolly and casually, or excitedly and enthusiastically.

Nearly every office supply store sells cassette label paper at competitive prices. When I have time, I produce a customized label on my PC, such as "A message for John." If time-pressed, I stamp my address on the cassette label and send it as is.

What to say on your cassette letter? I start mine with the following script:

> *Good morning John,*
>
> *My name is Jeff Davidson. I'm a professional speaker and author. I'm sending you this message because I believe my newly developed presentation on handling information overload will greatly benefit your business. Recognizing that you're extremely busy, I'll keep my message to the point. . .*

I then offer two or three specific, compelling reasons why it is in the recipient's best interest to use my services or follow up on what I'm suggesting. The reason might include saving time, saving money, or reducing frustration. I repeat my name and phone number slowly and distinctly, concluding each message with: "Thanks for your time and attention." I then say "Yours truly, Jeff Davidson," putting emphasis on my name as I end this audio letter.

Over the years, I've been encouraged by the results of taped letters. After receiving my message, some people call or write me that day. With others, the following week when I phone to discuss my proposal personally, I find that the target's level of recall is greater than for a letter.

Before starting a taping session, I've already prepared the mailing package and any other inserts that will be included with the cassette. When I first pop the cassette into the tape player, I rewind it all the way to the beginning, then count 8 seconds to make sure I have cleared the leader tape. Then it is simply a matter of talking.

Sometimes I tape ten cassette messages at one sitting, using only one side of the 3-minute cassettes. I then proceed with my presentation, making sure it doesn't sound canned or read. Most times, I complete an entire 3-minute message without interruptions, but if I have to stop, it's no problem. I often finish ten personalized cassette messages in under 45 minutes.

HOT TIPS/INSIGHTS FROM CHAPTER 7

- Use your fax to transmit price revisions to customers, outline key points you've made following a presentation, or send updates and reminders, among dozens of other uses.
- Use your fax to review plans, proposals, outlines, and other client items that you can improve upon.
- Invest in equipment that helps develop information as well equipment that speeds its transfer.
- The fastest way to create the copy for proposals, bids, sales letters, and flyers is to dictate them.

- Use e-mail as part of a coordinated effort to stay in touch with and serve others.
- Use express mail when you have to, keeping in mind that it has seen its day in terms of consistently having high receiver impact.
- To achieve notable receiver impact at low cost, investigate the variety of postal services available.
- The outside marketing appeal of your packages is as important as what you put in them. Use quick stampers and other distinctive features to capture a recipient's attention.
- Use audio letters as a creative marketing tool to stand out among your competitors.

CHAPTER 8

Marketing and Desktop Publishing

Gutenberg gave the Western world the power of the printing press. Desktop publishing puts it in everyone's hands.

Despite all the breakthroughs in information technology, people still enjoy receiving hard copy items via mail and delivery services. In terms of generating your own intriguing hard copy to send to others via mail, fax, or e-mail attachment, desktop publishing is a personal publishing breakthrough now in a mature stage. Such a large volume of books and articles has already been written on the topic that we will focus here on simple criteria by which you can make good marketing use of the tools you already have available.

A MANDATORY REQUIREMENT

Clients and customers today automatically expect the best in appearance and layout of the printed materials they receive. Whether you use desktop publishing to produce end products for the client or use it only to generate new business, e.g., for your proposals, contracts, and bids, you will find that near-typeset-quality print gives you the image edge over letter-quality or near-letter-quality print every time. Even though high quality printers have long been available at affordable prices, too many home-based entrepreneurs are still attempting to "get by" with whatever printer is still working for them. Join the rest of the world. Sell your old printer.

More than a tool for creating new documents appearing to be typeset, desktop publishing affords you the capability of converting anything you presently have on disk for repackaging and reuse. Suppose you typed out the speech that you gave to the Rotary Club last month and saved it on disk. With desktop publishing, that speech can now be converted to a special report, opinion piece for publication, monograph, or newsletter section of near-typeset quality.

Similarly, you can skim through all of your files on disk to determine what new marketing-support products can be generated by producing a new layout. Think of it: a slogan can become an overhead, an article can become a small booklet, a letter to the editor can be come a position statement.

Brian, a home-based accountant, found that he could readily convert tax-analysis reports for specific clients into generic reports on how the new tax laws affect particular lines of business. By removing the names of the specific clients who had generated the reports, as well as any specifics related to their operations, and by further generalizing some passages for a wider audience, he was able to produce three reports averaging twelve pages each. He priced them at $18.95.

Using desktop publishing, Brian also generated a one-page sales flyer and order form. He included the flyer in routine correspondence with other clients and found that more than half of those receiving the flyer ordered a report. Obviously, at $18.95, he would have to sell several score to make a sizable profit, but the report helped stimulate additional business with existing clients. Some clients had been relying on him only for their year-end audits. A handful of clients called him to arrange appointments. They wanted to discuss issues such as how they could meet tax obligations, improve cash flow, and maintain a safety margin in working capital.

More Business with Nicer Pages

Elena, an independent insurance agent, felt that she could benefit by providing near-typeset presentation materials, complete with graphics, geared to each client. She could have learned to do this all herself, but *she was busy*, and she would rather pay somebody to do it for her. The first thing she did was to assemble all of the reports and documents that she felt could look better on the page. She then visited three home-based services that, not coincidentally, were all within walking distance of her office.

Always the prepared professional, Elena used a checklist with each of the services. Her primary goal was to find out how each would approach the task, how much each would charge, and the typical turnaround times.

She asked to see samples of work they had done for other customers and was particularly interested in knowing if they had worked with other insurance agents. She asked about the equipment that each used, including the type of software, whether they had fax and e-mail, and what type of printer was available.

Elena gave each service two not-so-hypothetical assignments and asked each to estimate the cost and turnaround time for the job. She was surprised to find that the cost estimates varied widely. Then she revisited the lowest-priced vendor to determine if that vendor's quality and professionalism would meet Elena's own standards. She decided to have that vendor do one of the jobs. She also asked for the names of references, whom she called. She found that the references were all pleased to have found such a low-priced, professional desktop-publishing service. Elena now needed only to receive her own job back on time at the quality level that she was expecting, and the selection process would be completed.

Billing Rates

Some services bill on an hourly rate while others bill by the page or the specific task. Billing by the specific task may yield a more accurate and detailed statement. You will quickly find, however, that an hourly billing rate is easier for all concerned. First, it eliminates unnecessary detail on the part of your service and a lot of trivial review on your part.

Once you become more comfortable with the service, and as it becomes more proficient in handling your work, the hourly cost structure will work fine. Most services are entirely reliable and honorable in their billing.

In rural areas and those with low living costs, hourly fees can be as little as $10, whereas in urban areas with high living costs such as New York or San Francisco, hourly fees can range from $18 to $30 or more, and between $60 and $85 for specialized services. Keeping the cost in perspective, whatever a desktop-publishing service charges is much less than the same job would cost at a professional typesetter's.

Here is a quick summary of the advantages and disadvantages of using outside desktop publishing services:

Advantages

- Saves countless hours of wading through manuals and printing reams of pages with errors.
- Helps you identify what it makes sense to have in near-typeset form.
- Enables you to delay some purchases.
- Avoids your losing time playing with formats and fonts, trying to import graphics, edit them, and so on.

Disadvantages

- You may miss valuable opportunities to convert materials to near-typeset form.
- Each time you farm work out of house, extra delegation time and effort is expended.
- You lack quick-response (same-day) capability to respond to opportunities.
- Your out-of-house expenditures can quickly mount up if you're not careful.
- You personally have restricted opportunities for experimenting with formats and fonts.

Owning Your Own System

If you already use one of the popular word-processing software programs and you have a laser or script-writer printer, then you have desktop publishing capabilities right now. Otherwise, achieving high quality output and professional-looking graphics will set you back about $1000.

When Elena chose to handle her own desktop publishing, rather than get caught up in the maze of software and equipment options confronting her, she used a process similar to the one she used when choosing an out-of-house service.

1. First, she identified to the best of her ability every type of task and project that she'd want the system to handle.
2. She spoke to several friends who already had desktop publishing capabilities but who did not provide desktop publishing services to others. She wanted to learn what features they recommended and to discover the caveats they offered. She found she could use her existing word-processing software. She was told to learn how to lay out columns and set up tabs. Occasionally she produced long documents containing graphics. Thus the ability to handle these also became a key criterion.
3. Selecting a printer was central to her pursuit. She learned that laser printers offering high-quality print were available at a wide range of prices. She decided on a medium-priced model.
4. Elena was even able to hire her desktop publishing vendor to provide training!

After getting through several frustrating but eye-opening sessions, she began to gain confidence and finally enthusiasm for her new-found capabilities. She prepared a five-page proposal format that incorporated each prospect's specific data. Then, in the months that followed, she noticed a decided increase in the ratio of new clients to prospect presentations.

What are the advantages and disadvantages of handling your own marketing materials in house?

Advantages
- Eliminates many out-of-house trips
- Upgrades image immediately

- Can provide customized marketing-support materials
- Can prepare high-quality newsletters
- Often pays for itself within months
- Helps meet customer expectations
- Affords capability for quick response to opportunities
- Offers a lifetime skill, once you learn it
- Opportunities for use begin to multiply as your skill increases

Disadvantages

- As with any equipment, foul-ups will occur
- Mastering desktop publishing is more than many people bargain for; a considerable investment of time is necessary
- Near-typeset printing capability does not improve the quality of your writing; *a poorly written, near-typeset document is detrimental to marketing campaigns*
- Each time you buy new equipment, a whole new installation and adjustment process ensues

A DESKTOP CHALLENGE: YOUR OWN NEWSLETTER

Let's explore producing a newsletter as an adjunct to your overall marketing program. We will proceed with the assumption that you are not in the business of producing a newsletter, but that you want to produce a newsletter to maintain contact with customers, prospects, and others who can assist you by sending new business your way.

A newsletter enables you to offer high-quality executive communication to customers and targets at relatively low cost. A newsletter is part of an overall effort to favorably and continually keep your name in front of those people who can reward you with new business or speak favorably about you to others. While you may not be able to call on all prospective customers as frequently as you would like, once a legitimate prospect has been identified, the newsletter enables you to maintain contact that will be beneficial for converting prospects to buyers in the future.

A good newsletter serves three important purposes:

1. Information. Inform your targets and other recipients about the important trends in their industry. What is occurring that readers need to know about? How might it affect them? Any information that you compile about your target market represents potentially useful newsletter material.
2. Education. Is there an important resource or new guidebook that your targets would appreciate learning about? By providing the name, address, and ordering information for available literature or other resources of interest to your targets, you will be regarded as offering a valuable resource. Consider using mini-case histories of how companies or individuals in the target market were able to solve particular problems; the examples do not have to be from your own customers.
3. Promotion. By providing your targets with information and educational materials, you earn the right to devote some space in your newsletter to promotion of your business. Candidly recount some recent activities or results you helped customers achieve. Also review the list of *Good Topics for News Releases*, for items for your newsletter (see Chapter 3). If you have expanded your services or product line, relocated, purchased new equipment, won an award, or spoken at a convention, include this in your newsletter.

A management outplacement specialist found that a four-page newsletter distributed every other month worked best for him. He maintained a low-key approach to promoting himself, focusing more on providing solid information that targets would appreciate receiving. He garnered many favorable responses from recipients.

Features to Generate Interest and Fill Pages!

Begin developing regular features; avoid the problem, *What will I put in the newsletter this issue*? Here's a roster of items that could each be made into a regular feature. Notice that each of the following may also contribute to the information, education, and promotion functions of your newsletter:

- *Message from the President (you).* What are the important issues in the targets' industry since the last newsletter? Also include personal opinion, forecasts, or other observations.
- *Customer (or Client) of the Month.* Profile one customer, focusing on something he's accomplished. You will make twelve good friends in this coming year by establishing this column—the twelve customers featured.
- *Industry Calendar (or Events).* List the important meetings, seminars, conventions, and symposiums of interest to members of your target market. This data can be derived from other publications. Nevertheless, recipients will certainly appreciate it being listed concisely in your newsletter.
- *Technical Report.* Offer a roundup of new equipment or technology that supports customers' efforts, or new uses for existing technology. Your assessment of the effectiveness of new equipment, its costs, and its potential applications will be appreciated by many recipients.
- *Interview.* Present a 150- to 300-word interview with one of the movers and shakers in the industry: association executives; magazine, journal, or newsletter publishers; key clients and client staff people; and other experts.
- *Reprints, Excerpts, and Adaptations.* Reprint information that first appeared in another print medium. You will have to secure permission, which usually is readily granted.

Here are other items that can keep your newsletter fresh, vibrant, and in demand:

- Cartoons or captions appropriate for your targets
- Indications of your availability as a speaker
- Synopses of meetings within the targets' industries
- Graphs or charts depicting trends in the industry, financial changes, and other noteworthy developments

Once you get started, identifying newsletter material is not difficult. You can assign a part-time helper the responsibility of clipping articles and keeping an eye open for newsletter items, from which you can make the final selection. Luce Press Clippings offers a free newspaper "slasher"—a small tool that allows you to deftly extract newspaper articles. For more information, contact Luce Press Clippings, 42 S. Center St., Mesa, AZ 85210, (800) 528-8226.

Whatever you do, deliver consistency. Assess each issue of your newsletter for balance, readability, and adherence to your company's marketing objectives. A newsletter that accurately conveys your business's goals and objectives is a marketing tool worth maintaining. Many entrepreneurs see their newsletters as an invaluable means of maintaining a continuing dialogue with customers and potential customers.

As with any form of targeted communication, your list of newsletter recipients has to be continually updated as necessary.

Size and Format

One- and three-page newsletters are possibilities, but have drawbacks. A one-page newsletter doesn't allow much depth of coverage of topics or features. Also, customers and recipients may not save the issues. A three-page newsletter—three single sheets joined by a staple, or two sheets folded over to make four, normal-sized pages with the back sheet for mailing information—appears a bit unbalanced.

Two- and four-page newsletters are popular and may work best for you. Two pages (front and back) or four pages (two 11" × 17" pages folded over) are simple in design and easy to mail. Beyond four pages, you have to consider the difficulty of maintaining reader interest and the toll on your own time. Hence, I don't recommend it except for the brave.

Three-hole-punch your newsletter to encourage recipients to save it. The popular page size in the United States remains 8 ½" × 11". If larger, your newsletter won't fit into notebooks or file folders. If smaller, it may get lost among other documents.

One home-based marketer distributes a four-page newsletter and includes a Customer of the Month feature. She prints 260 copies: 230 for her own distribution and 30 for the customer featured that month. The customer featured usually distributes those copies to his own customers.

Another home-based marketer issues a two-page monthly newsletter to clients in the communications industry. After a few months, people who had seen the newsletter were calling to receive it, even though they had never met the editor personally.

A Viable Alternative

In communications, as in other services, association-based and private publishing services offering generic newsletters are viable alternatives. These publications are written, produced, and shipped to subscribers (such as yourself) who then add their own copy, name, and address on the final page (or final two pages). The publication appears to be entirely their own creation. The cost ranges widely from $400 to $800 for 2,000 copies, with more attractive rates for larger orders. There are additional costs for the inclusion of more customized pages (see Chapter 11 for more on assistance from associations).

Here's a summary of the advantages and disadvantages of producing your own newsletter in house:

Advantages

- Fairly effective way to stay in touch with many customers or clients and prospects.
- Can be altered for a specific target group.
- Can double as press releases, articles for submission, and other marketing-support materials.
- A key item in the development of the distinctive image of your business.
- A potentially salable item.
- The discipline required to gather the information to keep its columns filled helps keep you current, sharp, and in demand.

Disadvantages

- Time consuming.
- Cost of paper, mailing, and part-time labor can be significant.
- Susceptibility to editorial burnout.
- If not targeted correctly, can be a terrible drain.
- Represents another task on an endless "to-do" list.
- Finding a typo in the first paragraph after you have distributed the newsletter is disheartening.
- You may be giving away advice you could be selling.

One-page "Faxables"

The one-page faxable or one-sheet is a marketing standard in many businesses. Some rely on it in a major way. The best faxables are self-contained: the entire message that the sender wants to convey is contained on a side or two of one page. Here are examples I use: The first, obviously, is professionally typeset, on both sides. The two on pages 142 and 143, however, were produced entirely by myself, at my home-based office.

Streamlining Your Work and Your Life
From one of America's leading experts on staying competitive, productive, and balanced
Jeff Davidson

Jeff Davidson, MBA, CMC, is a leading expert at helping people to live and work at a comfortable pace in a sped-up society. Honored with the Certified Management Consultant designation by the Institute of Management Consultants, since 1983 Jeff has offered dynamic learning keynotes and seminar presentations to executives and entrepreneurs in all industries. Three of his presentations are featured in *Vital Speeches of the Day.*

Jeff is founder of the Breathing Space® Institute in Chapel Hill, North Carolina. All told, more than 325,000 people have benefited from his books, cassettes, videos, keynote presentations, executive seminars, and national columns. Millions more have read about Jeff in *USA Today, The Washington Post, Los Angeles Times, San Francisco Chronicle, Chicago Tribune,* and *Boston Herald.* Others have seen or heard Jeff on CBS *Nightwatch, Ask Washington,* CNBC, Sun Radio, Mutual Radio, and hundreds of regional talk shows.

His 24 books, cumulatively selected by book clubs 20 times, and published in nine languages, include *Breathing Space: Living & Working at a Comfortable Pace in a Sped-Up Society* (MasterMedia), *Handling Stress* (Macmillan), *Getting New Clients* (Wiley), *Selling to the Giants* (McGraw-Hill), and *How to Have a Good Year Every Year* (Berkley).

Jeff combines outstanding high content with humor, flair, and inspiration, leaving his audiences supercharged and ready for action.

KEYNOTE TOPICS

OVERWORKED OR OVERWHELMED?
You can handle the quick turn-around requests or longer hours; it's everything else competing for your attention that leaves you feeling overwhelmed. Once overwhelmed, a feeling of being overworked can quickly follow. In this presentation, you'll learn space, time, and stress management techniques most people have not considered, as well as progressive methods for daily effectiveness that anyone can master.

"Once you understand the root causes of the time-pressure you feel, control, and even mastery, are entirely attainable."
-- Jeff Davidson

STAYING CONFIDENT AND PROSPEROUS IN A WORLD OF RAPID CHANGE
No one in society has a long term lock on any market niche, and no body of information provides a competitive advantage for very long. Today's reality is that everyone feels at least a little unsure of himself, and in that sense everyone is in the same boat. In this spellbinding presentation, Jeff spells out how to remain prosperous and confident independent of the frequency of change you face, and how to maintain a sense of breathing space along the way. If you work for a living, you won't want to miss hearing this.

"In a rapidly changing society, many managers needlessly lose confidence in their ability to stay competitive."
-- Jeff Davidson

HANDLING INFORMATION OVERLOAD
Data, data everywhere but not a thought to think! Does too much paper, too much reading, too many web sites, and too much to keep pace with diminish your enjoyment of life? If so, go from glut to gain. This presentation enables you to use information for maximum advantage, and keep the din at a manageable level so you can spend more time doing the things you enjoy. It also offers essential tools for continual improvement. The program is designed for organizations whose managers and key staff or members face a daily glut of too much competing for their time and attention.

"More information is generated on Earth in one hour than you could digest in the rest of your life." -- Jeff Davidson

Information about Jeff Davidson's presentations:
❏ Program emphasis, length, and titles are tailored to meet your needs.
❏ Meeting professionals often request one program as a keynote and another as a workshop or breakout session.
❏ Jeff has addressed over 400 audiences, ranging from 15 to 1000s.
❏ Clients: Corporations, Franchises, Associations, Government, Health Care, Professional Service Firms, Entrepreneurs, and Educators.
❏ Mixed, multinational, multi-cultural audiences in America, Europe, and Asia; job titles from all administrative assistants, to all CEOs.

Breathing Space® Institute   www.BreathingSpace.com   Phone: 919-932-1996
2417 Honeysuckle Road ■ Chapel Hill, NC 27514-6819   keynote@BreathingSpace.com Fax: 919-932-9982

Streamlining Your Work and Your Life
From one of America's leading experts on staying competitive, productive, and balanced
Jeff Davidson

The Mission of the Breathing Space Institute: to offer people alternatives to high-pressured days, without requiring radical changes of them or what they do; to provide the tools, inspiration, and support people need to meet the challenges they face.

Dr. Tony Alessandra, Author, *The Platinum Rule*
"When I want the answer to something important, I turn to Jeff Davidson. The way Jeff thinks things through ends up saving me energy, time, and money."

Mary Lange, CAE, Vice President
Independent Bankers Association of Texas, Austin TX
"You hit a home run for us! Thanks again for being with us this past weekend. Your message is such a wonderful mix of business and personal organization -- everyone was excited! Thanks for a job well done!"

Del White, Manager of Civic Affairs
Unocal Corporation, Los Angeles CA
"Thanks for helping me to throw my stress overboard! You were a real lifesaver . . . good thing you were scheduled early so I didn't have to carry it around any longer. I look forward to receiving *Breathing Space*."

Marcy Fryday, President and Chief Executive Officer
SW Houston Chamber of Commerce, Houston TX
"Time management theories don't explain WHY we feel so overwhelmed; your five Mega-Realities do. You have probably saved me more than $10,000 in hospital bills and added 10 years . . . thanks for our best presentation ever."

Pat Baughman, Director
Associates Relocation Management, Washington DC
"Your ability to excite a crowd and hold their attention, particularly at the end of several intense days, is fantastic. Thank you for such an exciting and informative session on *Breathing Space: How to Survive in a Sped-Up World*. Wow, did I need it."

Captain Charles Anderson, Officer in Charge
U.S. Naval School of Health Sciences, Portsmouth VA
"Fantastic presentation to the HCAT members! I've experienced many sessions of this general type, but yours was truly unique. You covered a surprising variety of issues with ease. The day was most well spent for me."

Stew Leonard, Chairman
Stew Leonard's Groceries, Norwalk CT
"Best of the convention."

Beverly D. Wilson, Program Director
Society of Government Meeting Planners, Raleigh NC
"Excellent! Fantastic! Best SGMP meeting yet! These are just a few of the comments from those who attended your presentation . . . Several members began implementing your ideas within days after your speech . . . In closing, I'll share a comment from one of the members, 'Mr. Davidson was by far the most effective speaker I've ever heard!'"

Partial List of Clients

CORPORATIONS
Swissotel
Dollar Rent-a-Car
Allied Signal UOP
Westinghouse IRD Group
Cardinal Health Distributors
American Express
Homes for Living R.E. Network
Proserv, Inc.
Hughes Broadcast Partners
Landis Group
Gilbarco
Telecommunication Technology
    Corporation

FINANCIAL
Independent Bankers of Texas
Wisconsin League of Financial
    Savings Institutes
Indiana CPA Society
Independent Insurance Agents
    of Michigan
North Carolina Society of CPAs
Illinois Community Bankers
Independent Bankers of America
Washington D.C. Institute of
    Certified Public Accountants
Indep. Accountants of Michigan
National Association of Realtors
Community Bankers of Georgia
Tennessee Realtors Association

HEALTH
Carolinas Medical Center
American Speech-Language
    Hearing Association
Illinois Healthcare Association
Washington, D.C. Dental Society
Nebraska Medical Group
    Managers Association
Healthcare Executives Tidewater
Midwest Medical Group Managers
    Association

GOVERNMENT
Internal Revenue Service
Small Business Administration
U.S. Treasury Executives Institute
D.C. Energy Extension Service
Society of Govt. Meeting Planners
U.S. Comptroller of the Currency
National Institutes of Health
Women in Government Relations
Arlington County, Virginia

LONG DISTANCE LEARNING
National Technical University
Automotive Satellite Training
    Network
University of Southern California
Colorado Soc. of Public Accountants
Network Northeastern
Westcott Communications
    Project Workplace

PROFESSIONAL/ASSOCIATION
Employee Relocation Council
American Marketing Association
Professional Secretaries International
Society of Telemarketing Consultants
Washington Ed. Press Association
District of Columbia Bar
Councilor Buchanan & Mitchell
Alexandria Bar Association
National Association of Legal
    Secretaries
Society for Marketing Professional
    Services
National Rural Electric
    Co-operatives Association
International Association of
    Exposition Managers
American Society of Personal
    Administrators
Greater Washington Military
    Club Managers Association

CHAMBER/CIVIC
SW Houston Chamber of Commerce
San Francisco Convention and
    Visitors Bureau
Texas Chamber of Commerce
    Executives
Galleria Chamber of Commerce

ENTREPRENEURIAL
National Association for Paint and
    Wall Covering
National Association of Pizza Store
    Owners
Northern Virginia Associated
    Builders and Contractors
Virginia Electrical Contractors
National Association of Women
    Business Owners

TRAVEL/RESORT
Crystal Harmony
Marriott Hotels
Celebrity Horizon and Meridian
Crown Monarch
Coolfont Resort, Conference
    Center, and Spa
Island and Crown Princess

EDUCATION
Duke University
George Washington University
GWU, MBA Program
Martin Luther King, Jr. Library
Omicron Delta Epsilon
First Class of Washington, D.C.
Quinnebaug Community College
Future Business Leaders of Amer.
Open University
Connecticut College
Southfield Michigan Library
    Association
University of Connecticut

Breathing Space® Institute
2417 Honeysuckle Road ■ Chapel Hill, NC 27514-6819

www.BreathingSpace.com   Phone: 919-932-1996
keynote@BreathingSpace.com   Fax: 919-932-9982

Jeff Davidson

Seminars, Keynotes, and Breakouts

Managing Multiple Priorities

We live in an era of belt-tightening, where shrinking budgets are a long-term, not a cyclical phenomenon. Many executives and career professionals today are asked and expected to do more, while not having access to any additional resources. Such efforts can take their toll. Learn a variety of innovative ways to achieve high productivity and notable results, while maintaining balance:

☐ Manage multiple priorities with greater ease;
☐ Employ hand tools, power tools, and cerebral tools;
☐ Benefit from the multiple-priority grid system;
☐ Condition your environment; ... and More .

Marketing in Complex Times

Marketing effectively in the face of ever-present change is a supreme challenge. Becoming more proficient at reaching targets requires an understanding of how markets are being impacted by the Five "Mega-Realities" of our era: *Population, Information, Media Growth, Paper,* and an *Overabundance of Choices.* Gain new perspectives and learn the *Breathing Space®* approach to:

✔ Marketing your business, product, or service;
✔ Creating new markets;
✔ Influencing others; and
✔ More readily attracting clients and customers.

Creating More Space & Time in Your Life

Merely *living* in America today and participating in society guarantee that your time and physical, emotional, and spiritual energy will be depleted if you lack the proper vantage point from which to approach each day and conduct your life. Learn the principles for creating the space and time you want to have, to supercharge and re-energize your life, both on and off the job.

Other Topics:

✦ *Handling Information Overload*
✦ *Choosing When It's Confusing:*
   More Effective Decision Making
✦ *Overworked or Overwhelmed?*
✦ *Managing the Pace with Grace*

Jeff Davidson, MBA, CMC is an award-winning author of 25 books and a noted authority on productivity, self-management, and high achievement. Each year since 1982, his articles and columns on business, self-help, and systems for accomplishment, have reached a total of more than 12.6 million readers.

Known for his dynamic, memorable keynotes, Jeff focuses on issues in his widely acclaimed book, *Breathing Space: Living and Working at a Comfortable Pace in a Sped-Up Society*, to help your audience members meet hard challenges they face.

Typical **feedback**:
"Best speaker we've *ever* had."
Beverly Wilson

"Best of the convention!"
Stew Leonard

"Your ability to excite a crowd and hold their attention, particularly at the end of several very intense days is fantastic."
Pat Baughman

JEFF DAVIDSON, MBA, CMC
BREATHING SPACE® INSTITUTE
2417 HONEYSUCKLE ROAD, #2A
CHAPEL HILL NC 27514-6819
919-932-1996 ▪ Jeff@BreSpace.com
FAX 919-932-9982 ▪ www.BreSpace.com

Jeff Davidson, MBA, CMC
PRESENTATIONS OF LASTING IMPACT

2417 Honeysuckle Road, Ste 2A
Chapel Hill NC 27514

800-735-1994
919-932-1996
919-932-9982 Fax

www.JeffDavidson.com
jeff@BreSpace.com

"Your ability to excite an audience and hold their attention, particularly at the end of several very intense days, is fantastic."
-- Pat Baughman
ERC Conference

Having the *Right* Speaker Makes All the Difference in the World and in *Your* Program

Jeff Davidson is an award-winning author of 25 books and a noted authority on executive excellence, productivity, and high achievement.

Known for his dynamic, memorable keynotes, Jeff focuses on issues in his acclaimed book, *Breathing Space: Living and Working at a Comfortable Pace in a Sped-Up Society*, to help your audience members meet the hard challenges they face on the job everyday.

Jeff can provide keynote, breakout, and partners' sessions all at the same conference--a great investment.

CLIENTS INCLUDE: Swissotel, Gilbarco, IRS, Dollar Rent-a-Car, NAR, Allied Signal, Executone...

KEYNOTES TOPICS
❏ Managing Multiple Priorities
❏ Marketing in Complex Times
❏ Creating More Space and Time
❏ Overworked or Overwhelmed?

BREAKOUTS/SEMINARS
❏ Handling Information Overload
❏ Choosing When It's Confusing
❏ Breathing Space & Your Career
❏ Managing the Pace with Grace[tm]

A NOTE FROM JEFF
"My goal in addressing your group is to have each participant involved in the *whole session*. I'll work with you to ensure that your group is *entertained, informed* and *inspired*."

Winning faxables are authoritative, factual, and direct, but not pompous or exaggerated. The top 1/2 to 3/4 inch or so of the page is left clear to allow for the sender's "terminal identification" line to print on the receiver's end. There is little wasted space on the sheet, although it's vital not to clutter the page with print and overwhelm the recipient.

Faxables that support your promotional efforts will, by design, reprint well in black and white on photocopiers as well as other fax machines. Color, as a rule, is not desirable. Also, if you didn't design your logo with fax transmissions in mind, you may find that your logo doesn't transmit well at all. To get a reasonable idea of what your faxable looks like to the receiver, send one to yourself, or, easier still, simply copy it using your fax machine's copy function.

Here's a quick list of *don'ts* when it comes to faxables:

- Loud, garish print or claims
- Wasted space
- Lengthiness
- Nonspecific target

Fax in combination

As with nearly all of the home-based marketing and promotion that you do, effective follow-up using faxables is crucial. Ideally, faxables are used only as reinforcement, such as before or after a marketing call or mailing.

Here's a useful maxim: Even if prospects are greatly interested in your promotional literature and what you have to offer, they're not likely to take action and call you, because of everything else competing for their attention!

DESKTOP-PUBLISHED FLYERS THAT SELL

I'll close the chapter with a simple example that works well. A fellow speaker who delivers seventy-five to eighty seminars annually uses a simple desktop produced flyer as a back of the room giveaway. Entrepreneurs and executives seeking to improve their business-writing skills attend his lectures. The flyers simply but effectively promote additional services he offers.

A sample flyer, reduced and reprinted below, titled "Letters That Sell!" is self-descriptive. This flyer was printed on 20-lb. standard stock, in a light peach color to attract attention. Once and *only once* during the lecture will the speaker refer to the flyer.

Let us take care of all your writing needs

Letters That Sell!

Our letting writing service can help YOU sell your products, services and ideas.

If a letter doesn't get the reader's attention, it is never read and no action occurs.

Most sales letters do not get read. They are thrown away without being considered. Why? Because the author is unaware of the creativity which must go into every letter.

Let us at the Business Source save you time and frustration. By following a number of time-tested, precise, and proven rules, we can draft the letter that produces results!

Letters We Write Include:

- Letters to sell your product/service
- Direct sales letters
- Letters to arrange sales appointments
- Customer service letters
- Goodwill letters
- Letters to sell yourself
- Serial letters
- Novelty letters
- More, more, more . . .

Also, consider using us for writing your ads, brochure copy, and flyers. Additionally, we present training programs to help you understand marketing and advertising.

Don't agonize over writing a sales letter ever again! Call us now for a free estimate.

Joe Speaker
The Speaker Source
(555) 555-5555

Knowing in advance that thirty-five people will attend, he'll leave *thirty* flyers in the back of the room. Then, during breaks and at the conclusion of the lecture, the pile starts to diminish. When an attendee asks if he can get a copy of the flyer, the speaker says, "Why don't you give me your business card? I'll be sure to send one out to you." In this way he generates interest and has the opportunity to make additional contact after his lecture.

Regardless of the size of your business and the kind of goods or services you provide, desktop publishing is a marketing tool that can bolster your marketing efforts.

HOT TIPS/INSIGHTS FROM CHAPTER 8

- Review everything that you have on disk to assess which items can be repackaged and reprinted.
- Working with a vendor may be a time-saver for you.
- When developing a newsletter, offer regular features that recipients will anticipate, such as *Customer (or Client) of the Month, Industry Calendar, or Technical Report.*
- Develop your own one-page faxable so that you always have the essential information a prospect would want to know about you on one sheet of paper.
- Consider developing simple flyers if you can easily create at least a temporary demand for them.

CHAPTER 9

Marketing
Strategies for the
Innovative

You don't need a lot of money to market effectively from home. With a little ingenuity, and not too much effort, you can market effectively starting from where you are with what you have.

In this chapter, through case histories, we'll look at some broad-based strategies for attaining high-quality marketing mileage, including creating articles from existing works and developing goodwill or salable products. We'll also look at ways to combine PC, copier, phone, and fax to score big with prospects.

FROM YOUR DESK TO YOUR COPIER TO OTHERS

Like Adele (see Chapter 7), Gerald was fully sold on the concept of writing and submitting articles to publications read by his targets. He is a trainer who offers workshops on conflict resolution to departments and working groups within large organizations, serving several companies throughout the Midwest.

Gerald had much to say about the development of highly effective teams. Gerald also knew that getting articles published on the topics of team building, employee communications, and enhanced communication and effectiveness among working groups would help him position himself more firmly as an expert and sought-after trainer in this field. He used article publication in two major ways.

First, he sought to get articles published in the magazines and newsletters to which he knew his clients subscribed. These included the *Workforce*, *Personnel Administrator*, *Management Today*, *Manage*, *Management Review*, *Management Digest*, *Management*, and *HRD Review*, among others. With so many publications in this area, Gerald had too many targets to choose from. By scanning the following references, he was quickly able to assemble a list of more than one hundred target publications.

- *Working Press of the Nation*
- *Magazine for Libraries*
- *Writer's Market*
- *Magazine Industry Marketplace*
- *Bacon's Magazine Directory*
- *Oxbridge Directory of Newsletters*
- *Newsletter Yearbook*

All of the publications cited above are in the reference section of your city or college library.

Second, Gerald knew from experience, as did Adele, that even if primary targets did not see his articles when they appeared in print, or saw the articles but didn't take note of them, Gerald could make attractive reprints to be used as marketing tools. He used such articles in the back of proposals as exhibits, included them with marketing letters to prospects, and offered them as handouts at his training sessions.

Gerald was not a prolific writer and, like many home-based marketers, had a variety of tasks that demanded his time. Writing articles, in many ways, was a grind. He felt he would rather do anything than sit at his desk, stare at a blank screen, and begin a new article. Besides, he had to make money; there were bills to pay and mouths to feed. So, while getting published would be nice, often it didn't seem to him to be a high priority item.

Breakthrough on a Disk

One morning, while reviewing a proposal for a client on disk before sending it, he noticed that if specific references to the client were removed, a more reader-friendly introduction and closing were added, and a few other modifications were made, he would be close to having a completed article. He could call it "Six Steps to Prepare Your Staff for Team Building."

Gerald was excited by the notion of producing this article so easily from a nearly completed proposal. So he began reviewing all of the files on his hard disk. He wanted to see what other proposals, reports, papers, letters, and other items he had already prepared to win new business could be modified for his promotional efforts. On his first run through, he was able to identify six such files.

During the next eight weeks, usually in the evening when his mental receptors were not firing so high, Gerald fashioned six "new" articles, each on some aspect of team building. The articles ran between four and eight double-spaced pages, or 1,000 to 2,000 words. Gerald checked some magazine editors' desired word lengths in *Writer's Market*. He found that he was on target as to word length for most of the publications listed in his field.

At the conclusion of each article, Gerald prepared a mini-biography titled "About the Author." He pondered how he wished to be portrayed in this short advertisement. Thumbing through some of the magazines in his office, he saw that other article authors listed their town and state. They did so, Gerald guessed, so that readers could find them. In some cases, namely where the publication allowed it, the author had included the line, "For more information call (xxx) xxx-xxxx."

Each author's biography contained a short line that read, Mr. or Ms._____ provides/offers/delivers/serves as, etc. Some publications presented thumbnail sketches of the authors. Some included 2 1/2" × 3" photographs (wallet size), though most did not run author photographs. Gerald decided on the following biography:

Gerald Akins, M.Ed., based in Davenport, Iowa, conducts high-quality team-building training programs for organizations throughout the United States and Canada. He can be reached at (555) 555-5555.

That was it—everything Gerald wanted to announce in a short biography. He knew that many publications, even if they accepted the article, would remove his phone number. It was unlikely that they would remove the mention of Davenport or the description of what he did.

Henry Ford Would Have Been Proud

Gerald employed Alyson, a college senior who worked for him two evenings a week for $6.50 an hour. After Gerald printed out the six articles, ten times each, he then had Alyson assemble the sixty manuscript reprints on the dining-room table.

She stapled each one in the upper left-hand corner and tucked a reply label addressed to Gerald into each manuscript. She then placed one of Gerald's generic cover letters on top of the manuscript, accompanied by a reprint of an article written by Gerald two years before, which had helped establish him as an expert in the field. Each package was carefully inserted into a 9" × 12" envelope. Then, using a publication target list that Gerald had prepared, Alyson *hand-addressed* all sixty packages to management publications. She noted on a spreadsheet software grid who would be receiving what.

Gerald employed this mass-market technique because he did not have the time for or interest in crafting individual cover letters and tailor-made articles for specific targets. He knew that the typical response to an article submission is a rejection; he hedged his bets by sending out each article many times, simultaneously.

In the following weeks, Gerald received many rejections, some including the manuscript. After about 6 weeks, more than half of the publications had responded. Two of the articles had been accepted—one by a major publication in management and the other by a small newsletter with which Gerald was not familiar. All of the other responses were rejections.

Gerald gave Alyson the manuscripts that had been returned to him, and on another evening she carefully prepared new packages. She hand-addressed them and remailed the manuscripts. This time, of course, each editor received a different article from the one he had received the first time. From that second-round mailing, Gerald got one acceptance; all of the rest were rejections.

After about 3 months, nearly all of the first-round responses had come back. There were no other acceptances. On another evening, Alyson prepared a third round, submitting all returned manuscripts still in usable condition. There were no new acceptances from this third mailing.

Let's step back now and look at the advantages of Gerald's system for gaining visibility among selected targets by getting published in magazines and newsletters of interest to them:

Advantages
- Excellent leverage of existing resources on disk
- Small investment of time on his part
- High probability of getting at least one article, and maybe more, published
- Since finished articles are sent out wholesale, results are automatic, requiring little, if any, additional effort.
- The article-submission system never disrupts the normal workday.
- Because of mass mailing, Gerald achieves an accelerated rate of acceptance; i.e., Gerald hears from several publications at once rather than waiting for each one to respond serially.
- Gerald receives quicker and more helpful feedback; some rejecting editors send a form letter, others suggest the type of article they would like to see.
- Within the span of 6 months, Gerald will have three new articles published, and consequently, three more article reprints that can support his overall marketing efforts.

- Once a publication accepts one of his unsolicited articles, he has established a new channel for future submissions.

Disadvantages

- Although the article submissions are hand-addressed, editors can tell that he's taking a shotgun approach, and some resent it.
- Gerald's mailbox is often stuffed with rejection letters and returned manuscripts.
- Gerald has not made contact with any of the publications and may be sending something for which they have no use, hence wasting money.
- Gerald could be missing opportunities for publication by not making personal contact. How does he know which article best goes to which publication?
- If two major competing publications accept the same article at about the same time, Gerald will have to disappoint one of them by withdrawing his submission or getting it to accept one-time rights only (meaning they get to publish it once and have no other claims).

On balance, Gerald is able to solidify his marketing position, attract inquiries based on the reprints (some attract high-paying clients), and strengthen his proposal packages—pretty impressive results for not too much effort.

Here's another technique for using the PC to bolster home-based marketing. While the example presented is for consultants, the technique easily applies to a great many professional and business services.

USING WHAT YOU HAVE FOR CLIENT RELATIONSHIPS AND STIMULATING NEW BUSINESS

If you are a consultant, here is a clever and profitable way to exploit the power of your PC. It offers a wealth of advantages and is a snap to produce. Don Hauptman, a New York-based copywriter and creative consultant who specialized in the direct marketing of subscription newsletters and information products, used a customized memo or tailored report to clients.

Years back he had prepared a memo for a client in medical publishing, discussing the client's marketing situation. Then Hauptman realized that many of the points in the document would prove useful and relevant to others, once he deleted the client-specific references and made some revisions.

Ultimately, the document evolved into a twelve-page report that he called a *Marketing Opportunities Memo*. More informally, he referred to it as his wrap-up memo because he prepared and submitted it after completing a copy assignment or consultation. The memo outlined promotional ideas, ways to reach new markets economically, options for growth and expansion, market-research techniques, public-relations strategies, contacts, resources, and other topics of immediate or potential interest to the client.

As many consultants quickly learn, clients' problems are often more alike than different. Thus, while each specific memo required some customizing, much of the content was common to all. Hauptman kept a generic or shell version of the memo on his hard disk. Each time he prepared a wrap-up memo for a client, he retrieved the shell, then used the search-and-replace function to plug in client-specific references (such as company and product names). Then he made any necessary changes and incorporated original material that addressed that client's specific concerns.

Putting this Strategy to Work

Does this sound like something you could do? You bet! Begin with an existing client memo, or write one. Then strip the client-specific references. You now have a generic or shell document not associated with any one client. Polish it and expand the content, perhaps constructing a modular set of paragraphs or sections that can be included or deleted as relevant.

Customize the memo to the needs of the particular client. As applicable, use or delete your stored passages. Incorporate any new material that deals with this client's questions, problems, concerns, products, and markets.

It's best to wait a day or so before final editing because this will enable you to revisit the project with perspective. Then spell-check, copy edit, paginate, and print the final document. Give the memo a name that conveys a benefit to the client. If appropriate, market the document as one of your services.

Some of the material that you insert in a client-specific memo may be of sufficiently universal interest to warrant recycling it back into the shell document. Hence your shell memo is, in effect, in a constant state of evolution.

Here are some of the benefits of this strategy for consultants:

Advantages

- It adds value to your service. Suppose a client or prospect objects to your fee. Rather than submit to a cut, combat price resistance by making your services seem worth the cost. Enhancing the perceived value of your services sometimes allows the client to more easily justify the price to bosses, partners, or himself.
- It helps expedite payment. When you submit the memo with your final invoice, the bill is often paid faster. In selected cases, deliver the document only *after* payment. This tactic can also help speed the collection process.
- It creates goodwill. The memo is physically impressive and genuinely useful. It appears that considerable thought and effort went into its creation. Often it exceeds the client's expectations, and the client may be grateful.
- It stimulates new business. If the client follows through on one or more of the memo's suggestions, it results in new assignments and new revenues.
- It is relatively simple to execute. Much of the document is derived from what you've thought, written, or spoken about with clients.
- Some of the content may inspire an article, book, speech, or other spinoff product.
- Often, minor massaging of the text may be all that's required to target the material for a new purpose.

Disadvantages

- The remote but ever-present risk that two clients will compare notes.
- The memo represents the free distribution of a potentially salable product.

Single Focused Marketing Campaigns

When a marketing campaign predictably will result in one major hit, it pays to undertake the entire venture. Let me explain. When my eighteenth book, *Breathing Space: Living and Working at a Comfortable Pace in a Sped-Up Society*, was published, I began speaking to groups around the country on topics contained in the book. I would target national associations.

Suppose I went "whole hog" and assembled a hundred packages that included a copy of my book and my video, article reprints, features of me in the newspaper, letters from satisfied clients, and a personal cover letter to the target groups? The cost of materials, postage, packaging, and part-time help to assemble each package would run nearly $15, for a total campaign cost of $1,500. This is too costly!

Instead of sending both the book and the video to what represented unqualified prospects, I opted for a smaller package that included the *cover* of the book and the *cover* of the video plus all the aforementioned materials, at an average cost of $1.50 per package. One hundred packages cost $150 to send.

From this mailing, about five to eight people would respond either by e-mail, fax, or phone. Of those five to eight, one or two would book me to speak at my fee, back then, of $5,000.

Because my fee greatly exceeded the cost of the campaign and the likelihood of one major "hit" was high, the venture was a "go." Moreover, if the campaign had cost me as much as $500, it would still have been worthwhile.

- Clients may come to expect this added benefit after every consulting engagement.

It's best to include some type of note near the end of the memo that indicates that the items contained within it are *not necessarily exclusive* for each client, although large portions of the wrap often may be crafted for a specific client. Thus no client is deceived into thinking that he is receiving an original document prepared exclusively for him.

COMBINING TECHNOLOGY TOOLS FOR MARKETING SUCCESS

Here's a simple system for combining existing letters and proposals and the power of an effective telemarketing appeal. Let's examine this effective marketing system through the eyes of Phil, a personal financial advisor focusing on business owners and professionals.

Phone-Fax-Mail Marketing System

1. Call a prospect and introduce an idea.
2. Immediately fax some descriptive material.
   —Suggest it during the call.
   —Get them to want it.
3. Send a proposal by mail.
   —Have envelope and proposal ready to go.
   —Enclose return envelope for prospect's business card.
4. Call as promised to ensure prospect received mailing.
   —No pressure, just professional follow-up.
   —Schedule appointment, if possible.
   —If prospect is not in, leave clear message.
5. Second fax—endorsement letters or supporting article.
   —Use arrows and boxes for emphasis where needed.

6. Second mailing—more info; keep moving forward.
   —Use #10 envelope, distinctive stamp. Post-it note saying, "FYI."
7. Call again to schedule appointment or classify for future contact.
   —Meet initially at prospect's place.
   —Meet second time at your place.

To identify prospective clients, Phil uses several methods, including referrals made by satisfied existing clients; purchase or development of targeted prospect lists; attendance at community, civic, social, and professional meetings; and keeping up high visibility in his community. From his home-based office in the den of his 1,600-square-foot condominium outside of Stamford, Connecticut, each Wednesday morning, like clockwork, Phil undertakes the following steps:

1. He places three professionally produced graphics, each illustrating some vital point he will be making to prospects (single hard-copy sheets), near his fax machine.
2. To the right of his desk he places twelve *hand-stamped* envelopes. Under the envelopes, he places twelve, four-page mini-proposals that he has individually printed out days before. Each packet is assembled with a paper clip, not a staple.
3. Near the mini-proposals he places the twelve self-addressed stamped envelopes that include the message, "Please send your business card," in the lower left-hand corner.
4. He turns on his computer and selects the file containing the mini-proposal and a cover letter he has temporarily left unaddressed.
5. He places the prospect list before him. He has already printed his notes about each of these prospects on his database software; i.e., who referred each, the type of

business or profession—anything he knows about them. He knows that the prospects make a certain level of income and are sophisticated enough to want to protect their assets. Hence, he feels fairly certain, and has confirmed through experience, that the people he calls could benefit from his services.

6. As 9:15 a.m. approaches, Phil puts on his telephone headset and calls the first person on his list. If the prospect is not in or is otherwise unavailable, Phil goes to the next prospect. He does his best not to leave a message; the number of return calls he receives is far less than ten percent.

Contact!

When making contact with a target, this is how Phil handles the telephone conversation:

"This is Phil Michaels calling for Tom Rankin." Sometimes he forgets to say his own name and simply says: "Tom Rankin, please." Invariably the receptionist says, "Who shall I say is calling?" and Phil answers.

Often the receptionist says "With what company?" Rather than reveal his profession and his reason for calling, Phil says, "Mr. _____ suggested that I give Tom a call." On occasion he says, "I am a financial planner, and Mr. _____ suggested I give Tom a call." Phil knows that it's vital to use the name of the reference or any other "in" at his disposal to differentiate himself from the masses of callers.

When he finally reaches his party, he launches into his purpose for calling without saying "good morning" or other superficial greeting. He knows that most professionals today are extremely busy and, while not thrilled about receiving them, will at least politely endure an unsolicited phone call if the caller is articulate and to the point.

Rather than always using the prospect's first name or always his last name (since Phil doesn't know what the caller prefers) he instead uses one of the following approaches.

- "Your friend Bill Jones suggested I give you a call. I've been able to help Bill to achieve XYZ, and he thought that you'd be interested in hearing about..."
- If he doesn't have a first-person referral or didn't meet the party himself, he says: "Professionals in your field currently face problems in the area of XYZ, and I've been able to help a number of individuals to accomplish ABC."
- When Phil does not have a reference, but has met the person himself, his script runs along these lines: "Tom [Phil uses first names when he's actually met the prospect], we met at the PQR Conference. I was the one who spoke to you about ____. I'm calling because I've been able to help..."

The One and Only Purpose

Phil's only purpose for calling—and this may come as a shock to you—is to introduce or reintroduce himself, establish a relationship, and try to solicit interest from the other party. He's not trying to sell anything over the phone, which actually short-circuits many sales.

Phil is only at the preliminary stage of building a client relationship. He uses the skills that he's learned in courses on telemarketing and by reading books and articles on the subject. He's found that he gets the best results when he doesn't rush the process that he created and perfected. Of course, he certainly will jump several steps if the situation warrants it; i.e., if the prospect wants to retain him immediately!

From Friendly Call to Friendly Fax

Phil maintains a caller-friendly attitude. To avoid keeping the prospect on the line longer than necessary, Phil limits his calls to 5 minutes unless significant interest is indicated. Then, during the course of his conversation, Phil refers to one of the three major points he would like to get across, the *points covered by the three graphics he has available for faxing*.

Phil's objective turns from introducing a potential service to getting the prospect to say:

- "Send it to me"
- "Fax it to me" or
- "Do you have something you could send me?"

Now Phil's system kicks into *high gear*. If the target has a personal fax machine, and the overwhelming majority of them do, Phil says, "Let me send you this one chart that I have right now. It's pretty much self-explanatory, and then I'll be back in touch shortly." At that point, Phil sends the carefully selected prepared graphic via fax. Of course, it's on Phil's stationery.

All during these conversations, Phil makes notes about what the prospects are saying. These notes can be stored on disk, but should be typed up only after the call so that the prospect does not hear the clicking of the keyboard. The notes serve Phil's needs for follow-up calls and are quick and easy to maintain and retrieve. During the conversations Phil also addresses an envelope, neatly handwritten, to the prospects.

Sometimes, Phil makes the next call, and the next, and the next, until he has finished his twelve calls for that morning. Or, he completes the cover letter on his screen with the specifics that apply to the prospect at hand. He then prints the letter, removes the paper clip from the mini-proposal, staples the letter to the proposal, carefully folds the proposal, and inserts it into the hand-stamped envelope. He also includes his self-addressed envelope and a request for the prospect's business card. He seals the envelope and puts it aside, going on to the next prospect. So, in addition to the fax transmission, the same day Phil sends packets by mail to all prospects with whom he made significant contact.

Just before mailing the letters, Phil neatly copies the address of each target onto another hand-stamped envelope for future mailing. He could use a variety of mail-merge and labeling programs to address the envelopes. To maintain the personal touch, however, he prefers to neatly hand-address the envelopes.

A One, Two, Three Punch

Phil has now hit the prospect with a combination one-two-three punch. He called, he faxed a single, descriptive, one-page graphic, and he sent out a mini-proposal. This being a Wednesday, the prospect will receive it on Friday or Saturday, or at the latest, on Monday.

Phil's cover letter notes that he enjoyed talking to the prospect, contains specifics of the conversation that they had that morning, and closes with a paragraph stating, "I will give you a call next Thursday between 10 and 10:30 a.m. to see if it makes sense for us to talk further."

When the prospect receives the mini-proposal so quickly after talking to Phil and having receiving the fax message, Phil has immediately made a distinct impression and established himself as a diligent professional in the eyes of the prospect, *even if the prospect never becomes a client of Phil's*—but many of them do.

The reason Phil says in his letter that he will call is that few other marketers ever write this and then actually call at the time they said they would call. The few people who state in letters that they will call rarely do. Because today every marketer with a computer has direct-mail capabilities, Phil knows that the people he is trying to reach are inundated with mail whether they ask for it or not.

Phil's simple proposal in a hand-stamped envelope following a personal conversation *stands out in a way that few other pieces of mail ever will for the prospect*. Phil is not loud or pushy, just direct and efficient.

On most Wednesdays he's able to make contact with between five and seven of the twelve individuals he targeted for calling. Those he doesn't reach are placed in the next Wednesday's file. On Thursday, Phil calls those targets with whom he made contact the week before. Wednesday and Thursday mornings are best for calls because many people are too distracted all day on Mondays and Fridays, have appointments in the afternoon, or are otherwise not in the office.

The Follow-up Call

On Thursday mornings at the promised time, if he is able to get through, Phil continues his phone presentation. If he detects only mild interest on the part of the prospect, he then sends a second fax message that morning using one of the other two graphics he has available.

On those calls answered by voice mail or an answering machine, Phil leaves a clear and distinct message including his phone number and the fact that he would like the call to be returned. Few prospects return the call. He also send the second fax to people in this group. A brief note accompanies the second graphic.

Phil then undertakes a second mailing. He sends a brief message on a stick-em note that says "For your information" or "Thought you might be interested in seeing these." He encloses two or three high-quality reprints of letters of praise or commendation from satisfied clients.

Phil never backtracks; he doesn't send the same item twice, unless it's requested, and he always keeps the action moving forward. Yes, he'll call to ensure that someone has received the package he sent, but following that, he stays focused on the added benefits of retaining his services or adopting his plan.

After the second mailing, Phil waits. By this time Phil has developed a sense of how receptive each prospect is, learned a bit more about needs of each, and uncovered how each likes to be approached. He's careful not to be perceived as trying to rush or pressure the prospect, but is equally careful to convey the message that he's a professional with a valuable and perhaps urgent service to provide.

Appointments and Classification

Phil prefers to see clients initially at their office so that he can eyeball their operation and gain visual cues that may help him in providing his service. It's also easier to persuade the client to meet on the client's turf since no travel is required.

Phil seeks appointments of no longer than 15 to 18 minutes, unless the prospect wishes to go longer. Like any good marketer, having established his credentials, a relationship, and a need for his services, he goes for the close.

Phil classifies all the prospects with whom he has made contact, based on the potential for future business. For prospects not willing to meet with him, Phil gains in other ways the information he needs to determine how to classify them. Many prospects are not ready now, but simply wish to stay in touch. In any case, Phil enters

In today's information-overkill society, break-
ing through the din and clutter of too much
information requires a carefully crafted and
orchestrated system of contact, follow-up,
contact, follow-up, and close.

all data soon after he receives it. Meanwhile, as usual, some
prospects aren't sure or can't make a decision, and others simply
don't accept or return any additional calls.

Quarterly, Phil sends out a management bulletin to all clients
and prospects, alerting them to changes in the tax laws, financial
safeguarding opportunities, and other topics of note to recipients.
He's thinking of expanding the bulletin to a monthly publication
and perhaps converting it to a newsletter format. Prospects with
whom Phil has made contact begin receiving his management letter unless they indicate that they prefer not to.

Following the initial encounter on site at the prospect's office,
Phil prefers to meet those who become clients at his office. He is
proud of his office; it contains a wealth of materials that he can
draw upon during person-to-person consultation, and clients gain a
well developed image of Phil's operation. This strong interpersonal
association prompts his clients to tell others about Phil's services.

In retrospect, Phil has created a simple system using his PC,
telephone, copier, and fax machine to establish and maintain systematic contact with highly qualified targets. Phil's system is
applicable for a wide variety of other businesses, and it overcomes
one of the basic problems faced by home-based as well as other
marketers: effective follow-up.

Here are some of the basics of Phil's system:

- Prepare all materials in advance.
- Call only that number of prospects with whom you can
  comfortably follow up and maintain contact.

- Keep the communications simple and direct.
- Keep in mind all of the other information and paper clutter that prospects face.
- Don't rush the process.

On occasion, Phil has experimented with using part-time help to maintain the system. It turns out, though, that he is actually able to administer this system more efficiently alone!

Using Your PC and Copier

You can use your copier to support your marketing efforts in many ways. When you visit an office-supply store, stock up on extra reams of colored paper including light blue, canary, light green, beige, and gray. Colored paper helps lend a special status to your message when used for copying a flyer or announcement or as the cover page or exhibit page for a client report.

If you frequently make presentations, you may already know that you can run clear Mylar sheets through your copier to produce ready-made overheads. Most personal copiers will also handle glossy or thick paper stock, providing you with alternative ways to capture the attention of targets. Glossy paper is particularly useful for article reprints; thicker, heavier stock is appropriate for announcements, bulletins, newsletters, and other messages. For short print runs, your copier may be more than adequate; however, for several hundred copies, it is more cost-effective to farm out the task to a quick-copy center.

Let's summarize the advantages and disadvantages of Phil's system:

Advantages

- Though labor-intensive, can be administered by one person
- Relatively inexpensive
- Easy to maintain
- Self-determined schedule
- Builds both long- and short-term business
- Fits in with other marketing strategies Phil employs
- Proficiency comes quickly
- Low stress

Disadvantages

- Requires a variety of menial tasks
- Calling schedule requires discipline and organization
- As with any marketing system, some prospects may not be responsive to the approach
- Easy to get off track, i.e., to skip a week or not make twelve calls

HOT TIPS/INSIGHTS FROM CHAPTER 9

- Be on the lookout for spinoff products, marketing-support tools, and information items that you already have on disk.
- Continue to develop an arsenal of marketing support tools: articles and wrap-up memos, as well as press releases and letters from satisfied clients and customers; all contribute to and enhance your overall marketing efforts.
- Look for salable items among the products you create on disk: checklists, how-to guides, forecast reports, market opportunity reports, proposal prototypes, and other products that may be in demand in the market you serve.
- Using database or contact software to retain information and build follow-up into all marketing campaigns. Anticipate the need to contact each prospect effectively over a period of time.

CHAPTER 10

To Greet
and Meet

*Meeting at the prospect's office takes more time, but
offers more clues. Meeting at your office offers more
control. In either case, make the most of your meeting.*

H ere is the million dollar prize question: will you be meeting
clients or customers at your location? If so, it is one of the
prime considerations in designing a layout for a home-
based office. Your office layout, or at least the room in which you
will meet, needs to appeal to them and meet their expectations, not
yours. Let's focus now on how to prepare for, receive, and handle
visitors to your home-based office.

The ambiance and personality of your business is colored
by your location. Prospects and customers will judge the value of
your services or products based on the opinions that they form
about your neighborhood, home, and office. In that sense, your
office greatly impacts your positioning.

The Stigma Is Fading

With unprecedented growth in the number of home offices, the
stigma of operating from home and meeting clients there is reced-
ing. If your home office meets an acceptable standard, many people today will be amenable to meeting you at your home office and
doing business with you there. These people include those who:

- Have patronized other home-based businesses
- Operate their own home-based businesses
- Suspect that you may not charge as much as your commercial-office counterparts
- Appreciate quick and convenient access to you
- Prefer to do business in a more relaxed, informal atmosphere
- Have heard good things about you and are eager to be served by you
- Have considered starting a home business
- Have known you prior to your starting a home-based business

Despite your best efforts, some people, before or after meeting you at your home office, will feel uncomfortable or uneasy about the situation. These include people who:

- Have little experience in dealing with home-based entrepreneurs and don't know what to expect
- Are protocol-oriented, perhaps having worked in large, formal organizations all of their lives
- Are highly critical or tend to make quick value judgments
- Feel unsafe in your neighborhood
- Don't get the visual cues they need to feel they will be well served

All other things being equal, a female customer or client is less likely to visit the home-based business of a single male, unless she has received a first-person referral. Also, regardless of how well appointed your office is and how adept you are at greeting and handling clients, if your general location and the access to your office leave something to be desired, you'll lose business.

EXTERNAL IMAGE

If you live in a high-rise apartment building, garden apartment, or row house, you may not be able to do much regarding the overall appearance and image of your immediate external surroundings. The personality of your business will be shaped by your

Assessing Why Business Is Lost

No entrepreneur, home-based or otherwise, likes to assess lost businesses; it is painful. Realizing what you may be doing wrong or where you botched it is no one's idea of fun. Yet it's a useful exercise to help close the gap through which customers slip away.

There are several reasons why you lose customers. For many businesses, customer loyalty simply lasts only until they discover a faster, easier, cheaper, closer, more enjoyable way of fulfilling their needs. Your ability to identify the handful of major reasons why you lose customers is an important step in retaining your existing customers and in increasing your effectiveness in attracting new ones.

How many customers/clients did you lose in the last 12 months due to the following:

- Not explaining the billing rate or service charge?
- Not treating the customer or client's problem as important?
- Over-promising?
- Failing to keep in touch?
- Devaluing the customer?
- Having inadequate equipment or facilities (Hint: keep reading this chapter?)

If you decide to call a customer you've lost, slowly and calmly introduce yourself. Rather than mention that the customer no longer patronizes your business, pose the question: "You've been a good customer in the past, and I'd like to know how I can continue to serve you." After that, let the customer do all the talking. He or she will either give you the specific things you can do, or will tell you why he or she has chosen not to return.

In either case, it will be a valuable marketing call because you will either regain a lost customer or gather information that will enable you to help retain existing customers.

surroundings. Prospects and clients will form opinions about your business based on what they see from the outside. Attempt to make the external environment of your home office as presentable as possible.

Unless you're lucky enough to have a home office with its own outside door, clients will be coming through the front door, and their impression of your home begins there. If you live in a free-standing house, keep your sidewalk and steps swept clean. Shake the mat or replace it. Make sure that your porch light is on after dark and that the fixture and bulb are clean. Your street address or apartment number needs to be clearly visible.

Here is a checklist to help you determine how others may perceive your external image. What steps (if any) can you take to improve your external setting?

- Parking—adequate, close by, well marked, safe?
- Outside walkways—clear, clean, illuminated?
- Lighting—adequate, useful, working fixtures?
- Safety—populated area, nice neighborhood?
- Proximity of stores—clean, well lit, pay phone?
- External appearances of other buildings—kept up?
- Windows—clean, attractive, shuttered, numerous?
- Awnings—fairly new, clean, attractive?
- Shrubbery—healthy, green, trimmed?
- Outdoor sign—visible, helpful, updated?
- Lobby—attractive, clean, protective, doorman, inviting?
- Reception area—attractive, adequately staffed, orderly?
- Hallways—vacuumed, well lit, well marked, noise-free?
- Elevators—working, prompt, satisfactory decor?
- Stairwell—clean, odorless, kept up, carpeted, well marked?
- Entrance doors—painted, secure knob, well marked?

INTERNAL IMAGE

Once inside your home or apartment, prospects and clients will make immediate judgments about the internal decor. Some people say you never get a second chance to make your first impression. In any case, people who visit your home office will form opinions about many aspects of your home. The crack on the wall that you've all but forgotten will be immediately noticeable to someone entering your home for the first time. How do you stack up in the following areas?

- Rugs—new, vacuumed, stain-free, odorless, color?
- Furniture—dusted, polished, coordinated, tasteful, comfortable?
- Condition of walls—crack- and chip-free, covering, color?
- Windows—clean, draped?
- Overall cleanliness—dusted, vacuumed, orderly?
- Ventilation—air flow, air quality, drafts?
- Temperature—too warm, too cool?
- Others at home—children, spouse, pets, friends?
- Pets—clean, controlled, contained, unobtrusive?
- Appliances—age, condition, location, color, size?

Few entrepreneurs would ever buy a computer, printer, fax machine, or copier, simply to impress a client. Few if any clients will check how much RAM (random-access memory) your computer has or the number of pages per minute your copier handles. What they will notice is that this equipment is in place; the visible display of these items in your home office can be reassuring to visitors. If your office is orderly and well appointed, but you prefer to meet elsewhere in your home (because your office is too small or you prefer another part of your home for meetings), you can still offer them the quick office tour.

If your office is a perpetual disaster area, you're embarrassed by outdated equipment or furnishings, or you have any concern about showing your office to clients, then don't. The issue of greeting clients at home centers around whether it is practical to do so, whether it will favorably impress them, and whether it will help to generate or increase revenues. Close off, cover up, or move out of sight those rooms or portions of your home that you feel will be detrimental to your marketing efforts.

All the Right Moves

A few carefully selected items can increase the visual appeal of an otherwise drab office. Your chair, your rug, the presence of any shelving or file units, and what you've hung on your walls will be noticed.

If your desk or table is only standard equipment, perhaps you want to attract the visitor's attention with a high-grade, comfortable office chair. A visibly expensive rug can give your office an ambiance and appeal that signals to the prospects that they've come to the right place.

If you have degrees, awards, honors, special citations, and certificates, post them prominently in your office. They are office accouterments that subtly feed the subconscious expectations of visitors. Most people will never read your plaques, and it's not important that they do. It's only important that the plaques are in place.

If you aren't displaying plaques, go through your files and determine what could, in fact, adorn your walls. Consider magazine or newspaper reprints in which you were featured; letters from well known people, such as a senator, a talk-show host or an author; photographs of you with prominent people; and recognition from community service, professional, social, or trade groups. Three to seven plaques is sufficient; too many and visitors may wonder what you are trying to prove.

Working Wonders in Small Spaces

Defining the landscape of many metropolitan and suburban areas, the high-rise condo offers several advantages to the home-based marketer, though your office space may be limited. The sheer height of the building itself, at a perhaps well known location, helps make it relatively easy to find. If your building has a receptionist or a doorman, your image is enhanced.

Due to the design and construction of apartments in high-rise buildings, your office will likely not be near the front door. Most apartments in high-rise buildings are contained within one floor. It is crucial that your entire apartment, certainly those portions through which clients may walk, reflect the image that clients or customers have of people in your profession or line of work.

Clear an inch or two of closet-rod space in your front closet, and have several hangers available for the coats of visiting clients. Install an umbrella rack if rain is common in your region.

If you don't have the room to meet with clients or customers in your office, the living room or dining room often becomes the meeting room. That's okay, there will be no marketing repercussions as long as the actual meeting area is immaculate and all materials germane to the meeting are carefully arranged in advance of the client's arrival.

Meeting Where You Dine

Steve lives on the seventh floor of a fourteen-story building overlooking the Ohio River in Cincinnati. He's a career counselor who conducts workshops and seminars throughout the community. As a result of his lectures, he sees four to five clients a month at home. His office is attractively housed in a den connected to his living room with small double doors. It measures 10' × 12' and normally would be large enough to meet with clients.

Steve has an oversized desk, a personal copier, a flatbed scanner, a printer, and a fax machine as well as four 72" × 36" × 12" shelving units and a five-drawer filing cabinet. He is highly organized, spending a couple of hours a week filing and refiling information about career achievement, as well as client files. He handles his own bookkeeping, taxes, insurance, and other files related to office administration.

Steve knew that he could not meet clients in his office, and so for their comfort and his, he decided to conduct client meetings at his dining-room table. The four-seat dining-room table looks and is expensive. Steve always takes the seat with his back to the window so that the client has a wide view of the river.

Before a client's arrival, Steve makes neat piles of the materials to which he'll be referring during the session. He also has a tape recorder with an extension wire and several blank tapes already in place. Because of the fine furnishings in his apartment and the impression he conveys to clients when they first encounter him at his lectures, the clients readily respond to Steve's meeting set-up.

Beyond ample working space, Steve has found that there are other advantages to conducting client sessions at the dining-room table. Easy access to the kitchen allows Steve to be a gracious host, offering clients coffee, juice, and appropriate snacks. Both Steve and his clients are also able to stand up, move about the table, and fetch additional files or materials as the discussion requires. Steve's outer, hallway bathroom is easily accessible to clients—a key feature of any home office that caters to visiting clients.

When Steve holds sessions at home, he schedules them between 9 a.m. and 3 p.m., when his wife and fourth-grader are at work and school, respectively. Steve's sessions with clients are intense, so the fewer disturbances the better. He tapes his sessions and gives the tapes to clients on the spot so that they can replay the tape on the drive home. Steve uses both an answering service and, alternatively, a home answering machine, so all telephone calls are covered during these sessions.

Clients receive the full benefit of Steve's attention. With his equipment and files but a few steps away, Steve can readily get a key publication, reference source, or contact, and can copy the cover page or address and phone number of the reference, or other information for the client.

Meeting Place on Your Couch—It's All Business

Meeting with clients on the living-room or den couch is appropriate in many lines of business. If clients or customers visit your home, and you sell cosmetics or hygiene or health-related items (especially in the case of women selling to other women), meeting on the couch offers an air of intimacy and personalized service that a table or desk does not provide.

With a three-section couch, the easiest arrangement is to have each party seated at the ends, leaning toward one another, with the middle section used for the display, handling, and exchange of items. A clear, sturdy coffee table in front of the couch supports this approach to marketing at home.

An L-shaped couch arrangement is conducive to a wider variety of meetings. An L-shaped couch supported by a low square

If your reputation as an organized professional precedes you, and often, even if it
does not, many irregularities of your meeting
space will quickly be overlooked. Conversely,
the most well appointed, high-tech home
office will have only marginal impact if you're
unprepared to meet clients.

coffee table works well for many types of discussions including
sales, counseling, instruction, and planning. An L-shaped couch
fosters effective marketing interaction between two men, or a
woman and a man, whereas a straight couch is more conducive to
a woman selling to another woman. As with a dining-room table,
the key to effective presentations is to have all materials arranged
in advance of the visitor's arrival.

Separated by Your Desk

For all of its advantages in supporting you while you're
working alone, a desk can be a cumbersome space for conducting
client meetings. It's a death knell in a home office to meet with
clients who are forced to sit directly across the desk from you,
particularly if your desk doesn't have a lip or extended edge so
that they can pull up closer to write and make notes freely. If your
desk is not constructed that way, *do not force clients to sit across
from you.* They will feel uncomfortable, and whatever you present
will have less impact.

Similarly, within the confines of your home office it is not
appropriate to position a chair on the left or right side of your
desk so that the client faces you on the diagonal. This is reason-
ably okay in a doctor's office, where patients spend a few minutes giving their personal histories, and barely tolerable in
institutions such as agencies of state governments, health

> Wherever the meeting place is in your home, let your client have equal seating status, so that his sense of equanimity is maintained.

organizations, universities, and the like. In your home office it gives you unwarranted power and puts the client at a distinct seating disadvantage. Don't do it.

If you choose to meet with a client at your desk, position his chair so that your are nearly sitting on the same side of the desk or are directly facing one another over one of the corners. If the client does not have easy access to an appropriate writing surface, hand him a clipboard or other hardbacked surface.

AMENITIES

Beyond ensuring that you have an effective meeting space, and apart from your being a gracious and hospitable host, here are some added touches that any client will appreciate.

Coffee, Tea, and Camaraderie

Serving refreshments tends to make clients and customers stay longer, as does the availability of a bathroom facility. Whether or not you want to get them out quickly, *the longer a customer chooses to remain on site, the higher the probability is that he will make a purchase, and the greater the purchase is likely to be.*

Your counterpart in a commercial office has an automatic coffee maker and a hot-water dispenser for tea. Serving a hot drink to a visitor in a home-based office may be a bit cumbersome. Nevertheless, particularly if the client stays for 30 minutes or more, it's to your marketing advantage to serve him something. Why? As discussed previously:

By offering your visitors a beverage or appropriate snack, you help solidify the human link, which leads to longer-term business relations. Thus, appropriate cups and saucers, spoons, napkins, and serving trays can become important elements in your marketing efforts.

To avoid having too much to do once the client arrives, have the coffee, tea, or other refreshment in a near-ready state. Then, when you make the offer, if the client responds affirmatively, you'll have less work to do.

A Guest Bathroom

Though you may prefer not to, make the closest bathroom available to your visitor. Especially if you offer some type of consulting, counseling, or training, access to the bathroom is prerequisite to a successful client encounter. Take a tip from popular museums, fast-food restaurants, and other successful institutions which have found that clean, well lit, readily accessible restrooms increase business, period. Most visitors will never use your facilities. If they need to, however, be ready.

The bathroom has to be of powder room quality and freshness. The towel rack is to include two sets of matching folded towels. Remove all prescriptions, personal medications, cosmetics, and anything else that is no one else's business. As with any good powder room, your bathroom needs to contain the necessities, and a few niceties such as facial tissues. Always have a back-up roll of toilet paper ready and visible. Use a pump dispenser for soap, never bar soap. While you don't need to install a disposable cup dispenser, leave a few disposable cups out and available. Keep your wastebasket empty and spotless.

Marketing often boils down to one-to-one contact. One person convinces another that an idea, service, product, approach, or belief system will enhance the other person's career, health, well-being, life, or outlook.

Your Wardrobe

When not greeting visitors, wear what you want. Many articles in popular magazines advocate that you maintain a certain standard of dress, even when no one else sees you, because this helps you to maintain personal discipline and professionalism. Hogwash! One of the many advantages of home-based marketing is that you don't have to consume good clothing in the process. When working alone, wear what you like, what is comfortable, or makes you feel good.

Your attire when greeting guests is, of course, another thing. Yet you don't have to be nearly as dressed up as you may think. Even if you offer a professional service for which your commercial-office counterparts dress to the hilt, you need not do so as a home-based entrepreneur. You need only look successful. A sweater can be substituted for jacket and tie. Comfortable shoes can be substituted for black patent leather shoes. A woman might wear slacks instead of a dress. Do sport a Rolex watch if you have one, as well as any other personal items that convey the picture of prosperity and well being.

Clients, especially first-timers, may not care about location or dress, but they do need to perceive that you are successful.

To avoid potentially uncomfortable situations, let clients know in advance that dress is certainly informal. The traditional rule of thumb in the professions is to dress in a manner that matches or is one step better than that of your clients. The guiding principle in marketing from home is simply to transmit an aura of prosperity or at least to meet the client's expectations. No one except Ward Cleaver (Beaver's father) wears a suit and tie around the house.

Off Your Turf

The moment you step off home turf, "their" rules apply. When you head into the city or anyone else's commercial office, all prevailing business dress codes need to be observed. The dress-for-success mentality generally is alive and well outside your home office (although it is loosening up in certain regions and industries). You are king or queen of your castle, but on the other guy's turf you follow the other guy's lead.

SPACE FOR HIRE

In some situations, it makes marketing sense for you to greet clients or prospects away from your home office. You will want to secure outside meeting space when any of the following situations is encountered:

- You will be meeting or making a presentation to three or more people, particularly if they are from the corporate world.
- Your presentation will involve large-scale props or materials that would be unwieldy, unsafe, or inappropriate for home-based presentations.
- The prospect or client expects to meet in a corporate boardroom or professionally designed meeting area.
- Your meeting will take place early in the morning or late in the evening.
- The meeting will last for several hours up to a full day, or run over several days.

Avoid home-based meetings if parking is going to be a significant problem for visiting clients, if it interferes with your home life, if members of your family for any reason will be disruptive, or if neighbors or those surrounding you will be inconvenienced, annoyed, or disruptive. More and more states and local governments are enacting legislation amenable to home-based business practice, and in a few areas where there may be zoning restrictions, it is possible to get a permit or variance.

If you decide on meeting elsewhere, here are some tips to avoid having to make costly outlays for commercial meeting space:

1. Visit the building managers of the commercial office buildings nearest your home-based business. Ask if short-term

meeting space is available, or if they know of existing tenants with short-term meeting space or conference facilities that can be booked on a scheduled basis.

2. Check the classified ads in your city paper and neighborhood and shopper's-news publications to see what other space is available for short-term rental.

3. Network with other home-based marketers to learn of space they may have available or that they use on an as-needed basis.

4. Seek a reciprocal or barter-type business arrangement with a firm that is willing to provide you with available meeting space in exchange for your services or products. A marketing consultant in Tacoma, Washington, for instance, uses the conference room of a vocational school several times a month in exchange for assisting the school in attracting more students.

5. Investigate the conference or meeting facilities of clients with whom you have a well developed working relationship.

6. Don't forget nontraditional but effective locations such as library meeting rooms, university facilities, health and athletic clubs, and space belonging to other organizations and professional associations to which you belong.

HOT TIPS/INSIGHTS FROM CHAPTER 10

- Greeting clients at home, if it is practical to do so, can favorably impress them and help generate or increase revenues.
- Visitors will make immediate judgments about your internal decor.
- Client-proof your home well in advance of greeting your first client at home.
- Purchase a few carefully selected items to increase the visual appeal of your office.
- There are many advantages to conducting client sessions at the dining-room table. Likewise, meeting with clients

on the living-room or den couch is appropriate in many lines of business and can offer an air of intimacy and personalized service.

- A desk area can be a cumbersome place for conducting client meetings.
- When it comes to attire in which to greet visitors, you need only to look successful and meet the other party's expectations.
- In sum, you and your clients need to feel comfortable in your meeting place, with no unnecessary external pressures or disruptions.

CHAPTER 11

No Entrepreneur Is an Island

The moment you give up the notion that you're the only
one who can market the business and actually retain
some helpers, wondrous great things can happen.

Perhaps you left the traditional working world, among other
reasons, so that you could work on your own, undisturbed by
co-workers or staff. Yet, it often makes marketing sense to use
outside assistance. In this chapter, we'll cover several ways to
effectively harness sources of marketing assistance, including hir-
ing part-timers and using marketing consultants, SCORE counselors, and association services to assist in your marketing efforts.

"Part-timer" as presented here means someone you contract
with on a per-assignment basis to assist you with your business.
Part-timers can provide delivery, research, mailing, typing, and
proofreading services. They can make exploratory telephone calls
on your behalf, develop prospect lists, assemble data on prospects,

It's rare to encounter a highly successful
home-based entrepreneur who doesn't use
some kind of outside help for specific marketing tasks.

identify leads through targeted reading and clipping, and serve as sounding boards.

High-school and college students serving as part-timers tend to work at wages attractive to you, and many are quite capable of doing excellent work. Due to the concentrated nature of the work they do for you, part-timers often prove to be more productive per dollar than a traditional office staff person.

WHO CAN I TURN TO?

Students are just the beginning. You can also retain the services of retirees, interns from college programs, temporaries from agencies, and even neighbors and relatives. Many a spouse serves as a part-timer for the business of his or her mate. The cost of using part-timers is low. Many home-based marketers unwilling to pay dear dollars for assistance don't realize that competent people can be obtained for only minimum wage or slightly above that. A bright senior in high school, college bound, may jump at the chance to work with you on a per-assignment basis after school rather than become a counterperson at a fast food joint.

Students

I've found that there are 17- and 18-year-olds who are bright and competent whose only drawback, if you want to consider it as such, is their age. With the proper instruction, guidance, and follow-through, they can save you hours, if not days and weeks, in accomplishing specific marketing objectives. Students can run

Call the guidance or job-placement counselor at the local schools and universities. Most schools have job-bank coordinators who list part-time and summer jobs and maintain job banks and job bulletin boards.

errands around town, make early-round phone calls, make library research trips, or assemble data on your own industry or profession.

As many students continue to pursue business careers, the task of identifying and attracting a few good students need not be too difficult.

Interns

If you could have several college marketing students working for you, would you jump at the chance? Most universities have structured internship programs. To find out who is available, call your local universities for information on their internship and career-placement programs.

Home-Based Word Processors

Home-based word processors often maintain simple one-line Yellow Pages listings. Bulletin boards (the wood and cork variety) are good places to advertise and to seek the services you desire. Try bulletin boards at libraries, supermarkets, and schools. Then visit any local newsnet groups where people in your community may place "services available" listings.

Many home-based word processors offer excellent service at attractive prices. A home-based word-processing service, like other independent contractors you can retain, works on call; you pay for the services that you need. A word-processing service can boost your marketing efforts by preparing proposals, bids, sales letters, capability statements, or other written marketing tools.

Retirees and Other Seniors

Retirees and other seniors are capable of helping you in ways you might not suspect: market strategy, prospecting, even selling. Seniors can do a bang-up job of studying competitors' literature, using competitors' products and services, and surveying customers.

The Association of Part-Time Professionals promotes work opportunities for qualified men and women interested in providing part-time assistance. Their members include retirees, parents, women re-entering the work force, disabled people, graduate students, and others interested in part-time income opportunities.

If You Decide to Place a Classified Ad

An effective way to identify individuals who may be available and interested in helping you is to advertise for them. You can place blind advertisements (*not* identifying your company) in local newspapers seeking potential supplemental staff. You may be surprised, even overwhelmed, by the number of qualified applicants you identify.

If you need only specific skills for specific tasks, be fair and accurate in composing your classified advertisement. If you're in need of staff for certain hours or can offer flex-time work, emphasize the hours as a special feature. If you're located in a small town and you don't think there are enough skilled people in your immediate community, try the newspaper in the next largest community.

To compose an effective ad, simply model after the well-written ads you see, substituting the particulars of your situation.

Contact the APTP at 7700 Leesburg Pike, Suite 216, Falls Church, VA 22043 or call 703-734-7975.

In general, local newspapers (and some community shopper guides) are useful sources for placing your help wanted notices. These papers focus on specific towns or neighborhoods. Also solicit your friends; maybe they have spouses, relatives, or friends seeking opportunities for part-time income.

BLESSED BY STUDENT TALENT

Using the talents of productive part-time students over the years has brought me many benefits. Here's how I find them and work with them.

To begin, I produce a simple, hand-drawn flyer advertising the specific skills I'm seeking. Initially, I distributed this flyer myself, posting it on college and community-college bulletin boards, posting it on local newsnet bulletin boards and forums, mailing it to high-school counselors and job-bank coordinators, and mentioning to friends and relatives that I was looking for a student with certain abilities.

Frequently, more calls and e-mails came in than I cared to receive. I would hold interviews over a two-or three-day period, explaining on the phone before each student arrived that I work informally out of a home-based business.

Screening by phone is a breeze. The people you want to have assisting you need to be articulate, responsive, and upbeat over the phone. They need to know how to conduct themselves from the first moment you speak to them. Anyone who has trouble carrying on a conversation, has poor voice quality, or otherwise causes you to doubt his effectiveness is best passed over. Your time and energy are limited. You're better off not retaining someone's services unless you believe you have the right person. There's no reason to acquire a new headache.

On the interview day, I call in advance to confirm arrivals. If a student calls me to confirm, it's a positive indication of the type of service he or she may provide.

Upon arrival, I do my best to make the person feel at home. I ask to see his resume if he has one, a grade transcript, and any written reports or papers. I'm more interested in skills and capabilities, however. Everybody fills out a simple information form. I use the form as the basis of my discussion. I need to retain assistants who have a personal computer and e-mail.

Making the First Assignment

When students see samples of my work, they gain an immediate understanding of the type of work I need done. Discussion is helpful, but there is no foolproof way of knowing how the student will perform until you give him an assignment. Based on how the interview progresses, if I feel that the student merits further consideration, I issue a project assignment *on the spot* for which the student will invoice me. It's usually a one- or two-hour take-home

CONTRACTOR INFORMATION FORM

Name:

Address:

Phone:

	S	M	T	W	T	F	S
Hours
Available:

University:
Major:

Hourly Billing Rate:

Car?   yes   no
Computer?   yes   no
E-mail?   yes   no

Academic/career interests:

Where you saw my ad:

job, something that can be completed without extensive instruction and follow-up. Nearly all of the assignments I issue are done out of the house. I prefer it that way, and I suspect that most home-based marketers prefer it that way. On occasion, it's necessary to have the part-timer in the house for a couple hours at a time.

To ensure that he understands take-home assignments, I record my instructions on a cassette tape as I present them. I pause frequently and ask him if he has any questions, so that both his questions and my answers are also on tape. I give the student a pen and pad, if necessary, to jot down notes regarding the assignment, even though he will receive the cassette tape. I also arm the student with stamps, my stationery, and anything that he might need to expedite his assignment, such as books, magazines, pamphlets, URLs, e-mail addresses, photocopies, phone numbers, and addresses.

Then I pay him *in advance*, for several reasons:

1. I want to establish a relationship of mutual trust early on. The $12 or $14 I advance to a student is a small investment in the contribution he may offer. I haven't been burned even once on this score.
2. The advance helps the student if he has to make any photocopies, long-distance calls, or pay for postage. Since the advance does not represent the total fee the student will bill me for the completed assignment, he still has an investment in completing it.
3. Students, like entrepreneurs, are responsive to revenues received. I pay them on the spot because it gets the ball rolling that much faster and lets them know that I have work to be done.

On occasion, as part of the first assignment, I also ask that the student produce a one-page outline detailing how else he can contribute to my operations. This enables me to gain an understanding of his organizational skills (based on the way his outline is constructed).

Record Keeping Made Easy

I insist that students submit timely, fully completed invoices for jobs completed, such as the sample invoice shown. Time is computed to the quarter hour, and we always round up to the contractor's benefit.

CONTRACTOR INVOICE

Contractor name:

Address:

Week ending _____ (mo) _____ (dy) _____ (yr)

Job Name	Cost Center #	M	T	W	Th	F	S	Su	Tot. Hrs.
1.									
2.									
3.									
4.									
5.									
6.									
Total Hours									

Signature_____

First Assignment in the Bag

I request that the student make a return visit to my office following completion of the first assignment. I want to review his results and offer immediate feedback. If the assignment was handled properly, I issue two or three new jobs. If there were problems with the first assignment, I may offer a second. At times, my instincts tell me it is not going to work, and I ask the student if he felt comfortable with the assignment, what problems he encountered, whether he would enjoy more of the same type of assignments, etc. When it's not a match, it's usually obvious to both parties. So, as gracefully as possible I suggest that the student probably won't be interested in the kind of work I have to offer. Then I pay him and thank him for what he completed.

An All Star Cast

Now, let's meet some of the assistants who have helped me and explain the substantial marketing assistance they lend to my business. Both Erika and Jason responded to my flyer posted on a community job bank bulletin-board.

- Erika is 26 years old, with one year of college completed. She is employed full-time as an office assistant in a law firm. Two nights a week Erika takes courses at the college. She began assisting me at $6.00 an hour. Months later we renegotiated to $6.50 an hour. I retain Erika's services for about 6 to 8 hours a week.

  When I'm researching a new market area, she makes trips to the library and uses the business-periodicals index, microfiche, and microfilm systems to identify articles I need, which she then copies. She also does Internet searches and send e-mails to individuals who may have key information.

  Erika also compiles lists for me on disk and does editing and proofing of letters, memos, articles, and chapters. Because she is eager for additional billing time, she also makes light, non-urgent pickups and deliveries around town, initiated by my phone call. Erika lives about four miles from my home-based office and is willing to accept assignments on short notice.

Once you find good part-timers, you discover that the better you get to know them, the more they can help you. Once they understand your business, they can suggest new ways to handle problems and meet challenging goals.

Whenever I have a list of phone calls to make, for example, research to identify the proper contact person in a large organization, I give the assignment to Erika. There's no point in my making six calls to find the right party when she can do it. Then I have a ready-made list of contacts and I can call knowing that I'll reach the right office the first time.

- Jason is a Ph.D. candidate at a nearby university. He is juggling several roles, including serving as a teaching assistant at the college and conducting high-level research for me. When I need to become knowledgeable quickly in a new field, given 2 to 3 weeks lead time, Jason can assemble a package of the latest articles, download print outs of research, and other literature on trends and developments in the industry or other topic area.

  The dossiers that Jason assembles for me would require hours of my time, and I'd be resentful every minute I was working on them! With Jason, research is second nature. He gets $7 an hour. Each contract I have initiated with him has cost me less than $100. Where else are you going to get top-level, specific, individualized research packets for less than $100?

- Mandy is 21 and works full-time as a publications coordinator for a small publisher nearby. She also takes college courses part-time. Mandy did not respond to my flyer; a friend saw the ad and referred Mandy to me.

  When I have, say, a fifteen-page assignment, I usually e-mail the file to Mandy, who proofreads it, saves the changes, prints a hardcopy, and drops it off. That way I can easily determine what changes she's made.

  Mandy's instructions are "to be cruel." I need her input and want her to make whatever marks on the page she feels are necessary. Sometimes when she changes a word I change it back: I always make the final decision. She receives $6.00 an hour, and her input is invaluable.

A Continuing Cycle

As students graduate or leave the area, I lose their services. I always offer to give them endorsement letters, and many take me up on it. I've contracted with part-time students to help me think through marketing strategy, design a new logo, photograph me, and undertake marketing brainstorming with me. As you get to know your assistants better, you learn that one has photographic skills, another may be a master in the graphic arts, and still another may personally know that company president you have been trying to see.

Take all the valid advice you can get, regardless of the age of the source.

OTHER SOURCES OF MARKETING ASSISTANCE

Marketing Consultants and Your Future

Marketing consultants can assist your business greatly. Often, the biggest problem faced by home-based entrepreneurs when using marketing consultants is *not retaining them early enough* in the business planning process.

Why hire a management consultant and then not supply all the major information needed? You can't expect even the most competent professional to serve you successfully. Help them to give you their best. The more a consultant knows about your firm, including your weaknesses and blind spots, the better you will be served.

Why do home-based entrepreneurs hold back information that could be valuable to the consultant? Sometimes it's because the consultant is regarded as omnipotent; he's hired to use his expertise to help us. Yet he can't do his job alone. Your help is needed to convey the issues involved. Information that may seem commonplace to you could be a revelation to someone not as familiar with it.

Remember too, that it's a mistake to use a consultant only in times of immediate need or crisis. Marketing consultants can be used throughout the life of the business; they can help devise marketing strategy, accurately identify a problem, and determine how it can be solved internally. Consultants can help significantly when problems have been approached internally, but with limited success, or when new techniques will make a difference in your ability to address problems.

Selecting Mr./Ms. Right

Finding the right consultant is not as hard as you might think. In fact many sources exist to help you choose the consultant who will be most effective in meeting your needs. The Small Business Administration (look in the "Government" section of your phone book, or call 800–8ASK-SBA), local Chambers of Commerce, other home-based entrepreneurs, and university business departments can all assist you in identifying the right professionals. (A list of the SBA offices by state begins on page 225.)

Look for consultants who have earned the designation "Certified Management Consultant," a rigorous qualifying program of the Institute of Management Consultants. The Institute's Code of Professional Conduct is a useful guide in terms of what to expect of any consultant:

- The basic obligation of every CMC is to put the interests of clients ahead of his or her own, and to serve them with integrity and competence. The CMC will also be impartial.
- The CMC will guard the confidentiality of all client information. He will not take financial gain, or any other kind of advantage, based on inside information. The CMC will not work on sensitive matters for competing clients without obtaining each client's approval. He will inform the client of circumstances that might influence his judgment or objectivity.
- Before accepting an assignment, the CMC has an obligation to confer with the prospective client in sufficient detail to understand the problem and the scope of study needed to solve it. Such consultations are conducted confidentially, on terms agreed upon by the client.
- A CMC will accept only those assignments he or she is qualified to perform and that will provide real benefit to the client. But the CMC will not guarantee any specific result, such as the amount of cost reduction or profit

increase. The CMC will present qualifications only on the basis of competence and experience. He or she will perform each assignment on an individual basis and will develop recommendations specifically for the practical solution of each client problem.

- Whenever feasible, the CMC will agree with the client in advance on the fee or fee basis for an assignment. He will not accept remuneration from others or make payment to others on any basis that might compromise his objectivity or professional independence.

All told, there are more than 48,000 management consulting firms and thousands more individual practitioners in North America. As with other professionals you may retain, you need to check experience and credentials and compare them to your problems and needs. Here are some key questions to consider when choosing a marketing consultant:

- Has he worked with firms similar to yours? Get names and numbers! If none are provided, move to the next candidate, since you don't want to be anybody's test case.
- What is his education, work, and consulting experience? Does he have comprehensive literature? Does he have a descriptive Web site?
- Does he have repeat business with his clients?
- How are fees determined, billed, and collected?
- Will you get a proposal that covers all phases of the assistance to be provided?

Once you feel satisfied with the answers you receive and everything else checks out, feel free to proceed.

Score with SCORE Counselor

Today is your day if you've never heard of SCORE before. Operating out of Small Business Administration field offices throughout the United States, SCORE (Service Corps of Retired Executives) provides free counseling services, including marketing advice, through some 15,000 volunteers. SCORE Counselors work one-to-one with entrepreneurs for an hour, a day, a week, or several months. Write to SCORE at 409 3rd Street, SW, Washington, DC 20416, call 800-8-ASK-SBA or visit http://score.org.

Marketing Help from Associations

Associations offer another form of retained marketing assistance, although you may not have considered them previously. By joining one of the industry or professional associations in your field, you open yourself to a world of possibilities. More than 7,500 associations exist in the United States alone, serving everything from ice-cream makers to highway-safety consultants. Yet a large proportion of home-based entrepreneurs are unfamiliar with the associations that serve their industries.

Associations supply information that can be vital to marketing. Consider this: Many of the challenges you face in marketing your service or product have already been faced by others. Most associations have a library or publications center including books, pamphlets, videos, and other marketing-information resources available to members.

Many associations also undertake their own surveys to keep abreast of industry trends, growth areas, and changes in the marketplace. These findings are often published in the industry's newsletter or other special publication. The American Bar Association and state bar societies, for example, often poll members as to what type of marketing techniques they find to be effective within the confines of the association's code of ethics. Other associations poll their members regarding recent and anticipated equipment purchases and products.

Scouting Targets through Association Membership

Your prospects often belong to identifiable associations. Since many associations publish directories of members, usually available for a nominal fee, you have a ready-made prospect list.

A key strategy for you as a home-based marketer is to join the associations that serve your *targets*. In many associations, "associate" membership categories are available. So, you don't have to be a practicing member of a profession or worker in an industry to join its associations. Even in the case where there may be stiff membership fees, the insider information that you gain as a member and apply to your marketing efforts is often well worth it.

Wow! Every month you receive the same newsletter, magazine, fact sheets, bulletins, etc. that your targets receive. You learn their jargon, spot the trends, and understand the problems of the people you're seeking to serve. You are alerted to the regional and national meetings and other key developments within the industry. This is great deal.

You don't have the resources to be everywhere. Most days, you're at your office or meeting with clients, and you consider your time to be precious. The few dollars that you spend to join the key association of your targets provide you with a continuing pipeline of marketing information, research, and leads, all delivered to your mailbox.

Here are the pros and cons of joining associations for marketing purposes:

Advantages
- Single yearly fee.
- Marketing information delivered to your door.
- Access to online chat rooms, bulletin boards, and forums.
- Stimulates your creative-marketing thought process.
- Enables you to leverage your time.
- Membership directories supply ready-made target lists.
- Reaffirms your commitment to penetrating this market.
- Your name gets on the same junk-mail list as your targets, so you get to see what other marketers are attempting to sell them.

Disadvantages
- Fee may be high.
- You may join the wrong organization.
- You may receive more information than you need or want.

Two directories that provide comprehensive information on associations include *Gale's Directory of Associations* and *National Trade and Professional Associations* (NTPA), both of which are standard library reference tools. Your assignment is to pick a key group to join within 30 days.

HOT TIPS/INSIGHTS FROM CHAPTER 11

• With the proper instruction, guidance, and follow-up, students can save you hours, if not days or weeks, in accomplishing specific marketing objectives.

• Many word-processing services operate out of homes, offering excellent service at attractive prices. A word-processing service can boost your marketing efforts by preparing proposals, bids, sales letters, capability statements, or other written marketing tools.

• Retirees and senior citizens can help you with market strategy, prospecting, and selling, as well as studying competitors' literature, using competitors' products and services, and surveying customers.

• Seek to retain consultants who have earned the designation Certified Management Consultant.

• Call your local SCORE group to obtain free counseling services. (Most operate out of Small Business Administration field offices.)

• Join one of the industry or professional associations in your field. Many of the challenges that you face in marketing your service or product have already been faced by others who belong to the association.

CHAPTER 12

A Good Location

If your office and other supporting environments are comfortable for you, you'll be better at marketing from them.

A h, control! With the ability to orchestrate every aspect of your home-based office, your energy, confidence, and marketing enthusiasm can remain at a high level for years on end. In this brief chapter we cover some of the added touches that support your marketing efforts and focus on when not to be in, why you need to get out of the office to make the professional rounds, and how to take your office on the road.

To Be Elusive

The ebb and flow of effective marketing (as cited in Chapter 5) sometimes means not being readily accessible. This is a delicate matter that requires a bit of explanation.

If you are there to answer your own phone each time a particular prospect or client calls, you may convey the unfortunate message that you're not doing well. Others may have erroneous notion that when you're "not in," you're in important meetings away from the office. And you want them to think that.

Now, depending on the nature of your business, it may be practical for you always to be accessible by phone and to answer your own phone. Nevertheless, to satisfy the need of some to fail to reach you immediately, at least 1 day or 2 half-days per week, turn on your voice mail or answering machine or turn your calls over to your answering service even when you could answer the phone yourself. At the least, this strategy gives you several hours to concentrate on a project.

A Dynamic Home-Office Setting

Did you come from the corporate world? If you're formerly from the ranks of the traditional office workers, you know that change is part of the territory. You were either being relocated, having your office walls painted, or co-existing for weeks or months with a new office manager.

Changes in decor and office layout actually help stimulate the creative marketing juices. If your home-office walls are light colored, your office environment may not be stimulating to you. If your office is overly dark, you may feel drained of energy. From time to time, hire a local painter (or better yet an artist) to add pizzazz to your walls. Decorate your office with plants, and rotate them frequently. If you have a southern exposure, you can use curtains and blinds to create different lighting effects. In case you think these are only small touches, consider that when you're on your own, you need every advantage you can get.

> Effectively marketing your business depends on how creative you can be in devising strategies to penetrate selected niches, so vary your routine to stimulate your brain.

Sit across from your desk and work, on occasion. Realign your files often to support current marketing quests. Clear the deadwood, and maintain an uncluttered focus on what will support you, your business, and your family.

Get Out and About

Habits form quickly. The longer, more comfortably, and more successfully you work at home, the greater the necessity to get out of your office and reconnect with the traditional working world. Once on your own, it takes only about 6 months before you notice a diminishing stream of new input and ideas because you're not interacting with coworkers anymore. Yes, your clients and customers, suppliers, spouse, part-timers, and others you encounter provide some measure of new input. However, you need more.

Every two weeks or so, schedule a key appointment downtown, and make other stops leading up to or following the appointment. Keep your eyes and ears open to changes and developments in traditional offices. Visit business-equipment and office-stationery stores whether you need new supplies or not. Regardless of your type of business or service, there will always be aspects of the traditional working world of which you need to remain aware.

BE A SUCCESS ON THE ROAD

These days, your car can easily serve as an extension of your office and a depository of marketing tools. Let's look at some ways to stock your car to support your marketing efforts. Always keep extra rolls of quarters and dimes in the car, because telephones and parking meters eat them. Keep an extra briefcase fully stocked with stationery, pens, paper, envelopes, stamps, a calculator, and (if you desire) a beeper, cell phone, notebook computer, dictation equipment, spare batteries for each, and blank tapes.

To be especially prepared, keep a fresh suit and change of clothes in a sealed garment bag in your trunk. If you don't already have one, invest in the best cassette player you can buy, one with automatic reversal so that it can change sides without your having to touch it. Keep your glove compartment stocked with tapes on marketing and motivation and other stimulating, uplifting messages. Also use your tape player to review meetings and conversations that you captured on cassette.

If you experience energy drops because of low blood sugar, keep several fruit bars or granola bars on hand. Stock a comprehensive set of city and regional maps with the phone numbers and directions for using your road service, such as AAA (American Automobile Association), and your automobile insurance card.

Visit, call, or write to your city library to see if you can get a listing of all the libraries in your area. Then, when you need a place of refuge while on the road, review your chart of libraries to see if there is one near your next appointment.

Connecting with Your Home Office

Today your marketing efforts can continue unabated, whether you're at your office or not. What kind of work can you do in your office on the road? You can do many things and almost anything. Write letters, memos, and articles. Place and receive phone calls. Take a sales training course. Motivate yourself. You can do anything away from home that you can do in your home office, plus some things that you seldom, if ever, have time to do back home.

According to the American Automobile Association, the average American spends 350 hours a year in a car, the equivalent of more than 2 full months of 40-hour work weeks. The idea of working on the road is no more revolutionary than working in the home. Learning to work efficiently and effectively in your car will not make you a workaholic; rather, it will give you more free time.

Take the basic car phone, for example. You can do more than talk on your car phone. You can hook it to an answering machine, a voice mail service, a remote computer terminal, and even a fax machine. Cell phones can pay for themselves quickly.

You might say, "I spend all day on the telephone. I get in my car to get away from the telephone. Why would I want to disrupt the one sanctuary I have left?" Well, how many times have you waited around your home office for an important call? Have you waited for the client who's been in a meeting all day and whose secretary keeps telling you will call as soon as the meeting is over? Get up and get out.

Have your calls forwarded directly to you in the car. Meanwhile go make important contacts. Take a few prospect names and phone numbers with you in the car and make calls while you're stuck in traffic. Some marketers have had great success using their car phones to help them make exploratory calls. They keep their entire prospect list with them in the car, in hard copy or a palmtop computer, and when they happen to find themselves in the area of one of their clients, they call from the car to see if a quick meeting can be arranged. Often this technique works well because of the spontaneity.

Real-estate agents often can tell you stories of how they were driving a client around town to look at houses when they passed a house that was not on their list. The client would see the "For Sale" sign in front and say, "Let's see it." So the agent would pick up the car phone and make an appointment to take a look immediately. The initial enthusiasm translated into a quick sale that might have been lost if the agent had first had to go back to the office and call for an appointment.

One real-estate agent decided to buy a car phone after she lost a big sale because a client she had been courting was unable to reach her at the office and, as a result, went with another agent who had a car phone.

Conversations on car phones, after all, tend to be shorter and more productive than equivalent calls made from your home office. Why? Car phone calls convey urgency: This is an important business call; let's get down to business. In the car, phone calls that normally take 10 minutes can be completed in 3 minutes.

The more time you spend in your car, the more important making your car your office away from home becomes. As new technology becomes available and the prices drop, your productivity during time away from your home office can leap to previously unimagined heights.

HOT TIPS/INSIGHTS FROM CHAPTER 12

- Sometimes it's preferable not to be in. At least one day a week, turn on your answering machine or turn your calls over to your answering service, even when you could be available to answer the phone yourself.

- Changes in decor and office layout can stimulate your creative marketing juices. Vary your furnishings, work station, and routine for increased stimulation.
- Realign your files to support current marketing quests, clear the deadwood, and maintain an uncluttered focus on what will support you, your business, and your family.
- Your car can serve as an extension of your office and a depository of marketing tools. Stock and equip it to support your marketing efforts and productivity while you are on the road.

CHAPTER 13

From Now 'Til Evermore

*The future will be friendly for the home-based marketer
if for no other reason than affording the opportunity
to do anything that's done in a traditional office.*

Welcome to the year 201X. You're sitting at your voice-recognition technology computer, which uses bubble technology and is therefore a 360 million times more powerful than the old PC you used in 1999. Your combination 16-in-1 machine/copier/telephone/ voice mail message center/ e-mail/fax/printer/clock/ timer/voice unit/two-way video monitor/pager/scheduler/holographer/simulator is built into your wall near your desk.

Your clients or customers are located throughout the world now. You hadn't envisioned it that way years ago, but that conference you went to in the spring of 2007 changed your way of thinking and being forever.

You employ eight people but have only met one of them, once. She is your manager, and she supervises the other seven. Freed from time-consuming detail and what used to be endless clutter, from your super high-tech, streamlined office you make marketing connections throughout the world. Changes in the external environment, particularly in the banking industry and its use of electronic funds transfer, have made revenue collection instantaneous following the delivery of your service.

A highly detailed, expertly designed data base aids you in rapidly targeting prospects in real time. Your closing ratio is higher than ever, while the cost of marketing and the cost per new client gained is lower than ever.

Hold on: This is not the distant future; this is the approaching reality. The future is exploding with opportunity for home-based-marketers. Consider the following:

- Companies are segmenting their markets with finer precision and going after the tiniest of the tiny—businesses like yours. You can thrive under this microscopic attention.
- More people will want instruction, classes, and to be shown "how."
- Most people, particularly HBEs, are once again becoming prosumers (consumers who have some participation in regards to production), engaging in various forms of production and consumption within their home and offices.
- A small but growing number of HBEs are buying homes with a complete offices already in them. The "hoffice" is a term coined at Creekside Commons, a development started more than a decade ago in Stuart, Florida. A hoffice has a professional office on the ground floor with the residence on the floors above. New as it is, the hoffice has already spawned a new genre of mixed-use development—professional, residential, and retail—around the country.

Smart Offices in Smart Houses

Soon enough, houses will be wired to serve you in ways once unthinkable. Ralph Lee Smith, author of *Smart House: The Coming Revolution in Housing*, more than ten years ago predicted a new era in homes and work. Companies like General Electric, Honeywell, and Whirlpool have participated in joint projects such as the trade-marked Smart House.

The primary feature of the Smart House is the safety and convenience that it provides. Its closed-looped principle for energy distribution prevents power from being distributed to outlets unless the device plugged into the outlet has identified itself to the system. The system is also able to respond to shorts, overloads, ground faults, and gas leaks.

Compact, self-contained, wall-mounted control panels enable the user to control every device and system in the house, including energy, communication, security, and lighting systems, appliances, and audio and video equipment. One system can be personalized by the homeowner and stored on a floppy disk.

Other manufacturers are busy developing homes with automated power management systems that incorporate microprocessor electronics to enable the homeowner to become king of his castle.

Such systems provide a personal automated lifestyle designed to provide low-end, entry-level automation to buyers of newly constructed or existing homes, with no capital investment on their part. Such systems will offer the homeowner convenience, comfort, energy management, and security through the installation of nonintrusive devices that receive energy signals through cable TV, FM radio, telephone lines, or any other circuit.

Your Marketing Vision

A good time to begin preparing for your office-to-be is now. Consider these questions:

- What represents the most profitable target market for my business?
- How can I align my office now to ensure that I will serve the best, highest-paying customers 3 to 5 years from now?
- What is the ideal equipment configuration for my office; i.e., if money were no object, what would I install?
- What do I want to be known for?
- What has to be done for this to be achieved?
- What support is available that I'm not employing?

What steps can I take right now to make my vision a reality?

Appendices

ASSOCIATES

Marketing, Small Business, and Home-Based Business Associations

American Association of
Home-Based Businesses
P.O. Box 10023
Rockville, MD 20849-0023
(800) 447-9710
Fax: (301) 963-7042

American Consultants League
1290 N. Palm Avenue,
Suite 112
Sarasota, FL 34236
(941) 952-9290
Fax: (941) 379-6024

American Marketing
Association
250 S. Wacker Drive, Suite 200
Chicago, IL 60606-5819
(800) 262-1150
Fax: (312) 993-7542

American Small Business
Association
1800 N. Kent Street, Suite 910
Arlington, VA 22209
(800) 235-2398
Fax: (703)522-9789

American Society of Journalists
and Authors
1501 Broadway, Suite 302
New York, NY 10036
(212) 997-0947
Fax: (212) 768-7414

Association of Professional
Communication Consultants
3924 S. Troost Street
Tulsa, OK 74105-3329
(918) 743-4793
Fax: (918) 745-0932

Freelance Editorial Association
P.O. Box 380835
Cambridge, MA 02238-0835
(617) 643-8626

Home Workers Association
7235 Saddle Creek Circle
Sarasota, FL 34241-9543
(813) 925-1909
Fax: (813) 923-3597

Intellectual Property Owners
1255 23rd Street, NW,
Suite 850,
Washington, DC 20037
(202) 466-2396
Fax: (202) 466-2893
International Association of
Business Communicators
1 Hallidie Plaza, #600
San Francisco, CA 94102-2818
(800) 776-4222
Fax: (415) 362-8762

National Association for the
Self-Employed
1023 15th Street, NW,
Suite 1200
Washington, DC 20005-2600
(800) 232-6273
Fax: (202) 466-2123

National Association of
Desktop Publishers
462 Old Boston Street
Topsfield, MA 01983-1232
(800) 492-1014
Fax: (508) 887-9245

National Association of Home-
Based Businesses
10451 Mill Run Circle
Owings Mills, MD 21117
(410) 363-3698

National Association of
Professional Organizers
1033 La Posada Drive,
Suite 220
Austin, TX 78752-3880
(512) 454-8626
Fax: (512) 454-3036

National Business Owners
Association
1033 N. Fairfax Street,
Suite 402
Alexandria, VA 22314-1540
(703) 838-2850
Fax: (703) 838-0149

National Federation of
Independent Business
600 Maryland Avenue, SW,
Suite 700
Washington, DC 20024
(800) 552-6342
Fax: (202) 554-0496

National Small Business
United
1156 15th St., NW, Suite 1110
Washington, DC 20005
(202) 293-8830
Fax: (202) 872-8543

National Speakers Association
1500 S. Priest Drive
Tempe, AZ 85281
(602) 968-2552
Fax: (602) 968-0911

Professional and Technical
  Consultants Association
P.O. Box 4143
Mountain View, CA 94040-
  4143
(800) 286-8703
Fax: (415) 967-0995

Publishers Marketing
  Association
2401 Pacific Coast Highway,
  Suite 102
Hermosa Beach, CA 90254
(310) 372-2732
Fax: (310) 374-3342

MAGAZINES AND NEWSLETTERS

A Sampling of Magazines and Newsletters for Home-Based Entrepreneurs

Costco Connection
Box 34088
Seattle, WA 98124

Cottage Connection
Mind Your Own Business at
  Home
Box 14850
Chicago, IL 60614

Family in Business
Center for Family Business
Box 24219
Cleveland, OH 44124

Home Business Magazine
P.O. Box 401
Holland Patient, NY 11354-
  0401

Home Office Computing
Scholastic, Inc.
411 Lafayette Street
New York, NY 10003-7032
Home Office Connections
909 Third Avenue, #990
New York NY 10022-4731

Home Worker
1500 Broadway #600
New York, NY 10036-4015

Independent Business
125 Auburn Court #100
Thousand Oaks CA 91362-3617

New Business Opportunities
2392 Morse Avenue
Irvine, CA 92714

Self Employed America
212 Precinct Line Road
Hurst, TX 76054-3136

Self-Employed Professional
462 Boston Street
Topsfield, MA 01983-1232

Small Business Opportunities
1115 Broadway, 8th Floor
New York, NY 10010-2803

Working at Home
733 Third Avenue
New York, NY 10017

ARE YOU A HOME-BASED INVENTOR?

Have you ever come up with an original idea and considered developing it and taking it to the marketplace? Horror stories abound of entrepreneurs who didn't have the knowledge and game plan to protect their concepts, or who suffered needlessly for years before making the right marketing connections.

"Many creative individuals, particularly home-based entrepreneurs who devise exciting new products or concepts, quickly run into dead ends because they don't know what to do to make their concepts come to life," says Richard C. Levy, regarded by many as a guru of inventions.

Levy has developed and licensed more than seventy-five innovative products in the last 18 years. He says it takes special know-how, perspiration, and determination to get a product from the drawing board to a manufacturer. Working in conjunction with Gale Research Inc., Levy produced a mega-handbook for inventors, titled *Inventing and Patenting Sourcebook*. The book exceeds 900 pages and reveals key information on protecting and licensing inventions.

Walking the first-time inventor through the necessary steps to make his invention a success, Levy presents sections from how to market inventions, to identifying federal funding for small businesses, and the names of 12,000 patent-registered attorneys and agents, 600 venture capital firms, state-sponsored inventor-assistance programs, seminars, conferences, and workshops, plus the official patent and trademark office telephone directory and hundreds of publications and data bases useful to inventors.

The *Inventing and Patenting Sourcebook* also lists more than 300 university centers, technology-transformation organizations, and high-tech parks, 200 youth-innovation programs and publications, a complete index to the U. S. Patent Office's classification system, including 122,000 terms in all, and a complete list of patent depository libraries.

DIRECTORIES OF DISTINCTION

The following useful directories can be found in most libraries.

AT&T Toll Free Directory, published by AT&T, Bridgewater, NJ.

Two sections including the toll-free consumer white pages, which contain alphabetical listings by name of businesses, organizations, and government agencies, providing toll-free numbers. The consumer Yellow Pages index lists the products and service categories.

Bacon's Magazine Directory, published by Bacon Publishing Company, Chicago, IL. Two-volume media guide to magazines and newspapers in the United States and Canada, containing listings of more than 10,000 business, trade, industrial, consumer, and farm publications. Provides information on which publications include new-product news, trade literature, general news, personnel news, coming events, byline articles, staff articles, letters to the editor, questions and answers, and book reviews.

Business Control Atlas, published by American Map Corporation, Maspeth, New York. Provides tables, charts, and maps of the United States and its population. Provides specific data on markets such as baby-boomers, blacks, Hispanics, children, and grey markets (broken down by age group).

Directories in Print, published by Gale Research Inc., Detroit, MI. An annotated guide to more than 10,000 business and industrial directories, professional and scientific rosters, directory data bases, and other lists and guides published in the United States that are national or regional in scope.

Directory of Conventions, published by Successful Meetings, Bill Communications, Inc., New York. A roster of 20,000 events, including business, professional, and special-interest areas arranged by geography, chronology, industry, and alphabet. Provides information on the name of the group, where it meets, how many people will attend, name of the meeting planner, phone number, and date.

Business Information Sources, published by Gale Research Inc., Detroit, MI. Name, address, phone number, and citation on more than 9,000 different organizations, publishers, and institutions providing business information resources.

Facsimile User's Directory, published by Monitoring Publishing Company, New York, NY. A 100-percent-verified fax number phone book, listing fax numbers for corporate headquarters of business and financial institutions, law and accounting firms, media and publishing companies, advertising and public-relations firms, federal and state agencies, nonprofit organizations, professional and trade associations, and leading foreign companies.

Gale's Encyclopedia of Associations, published by Gale Research Inc., Detroit, MI. A four-volume set describing more than 22,000 active associations, organizations, clubs, and other nonprofit membership groups in every field of human endeavor. Volumes arranged by national organizations of the United States, geographic and executive indexes, new associations and projects, and international organizations. Also provides two periodical issues of updated information for associations listed in volume one.

Gebbie Press All-In-One Directory, published by Gebbie Press, New Paltz, NY. Provides name, address, and phone number, name of editor, number of subscribers, and description of audience for ten major fields including daily newspapers, weekly newspapers, AM and FM radio stations, television stations, consumer magazines, business papers, trade press, black and Hispanic press and radio, farm publications, and news syndicates.

Manhattan Yellow Pages, published by NYNEX, New York, NY. A useful tool for home-based entrepreneurs worldwide. Manhattan is either home to or contains a sales office for hundreds and hundreds of major companies in fields such as publishing, recording, finance, insurance, banking, fashion, consulting, etc.

National Directory of Magazines, published by Oxbridge Communications, New York, NY. Lists all large and small U. S.

magazines including description of publication, staff, advertising rates, circulation, and competitive analysis.

National Trade and Professional Associations, published by Columbia Books Inc., Washington, DC. Covers at least 7,000 active national trade and professional associations and labor unions, including the year founded, the name of the executive director, number of members, staff size, annual budget, historical note, names of publications, and date, place, and expected attendance at the annual meeting.

Oxbridge Directory of Newsletters, published by Oxbridge Communications Inc., New York. Lists more than 15,000 newsletters, including title, publisher, address, telephone number, editor, description of editorial content, year established, frequency, circulation, average number of pages, and (particularly important to home-based marketers) rental cost of mailing lists.

State and Regional Associations, published by Columbia Books Inc., Washington, DC. Companion volume to the national edition contains listing of 5,000 major trade associations, professional societies, and labor organizations with state or regional constituencies.

GLOSSARY

Action letter (or **management letter**) A targeted letter sent on your letterhead to a client or prospect, suggesting that you meet to discuss a new product or service idea.

Barter The exchange of goods and services between parties in lieu of cash.

Client Anyone who buys a business's products or services.

Customer Anyone who buys a business's products or services. The primary factor and most crucial element in the existence of a business. A person or group with potentially unmet needs.

Customer service Satisfying and assisting consumers by various means including offering technical assistance, handling grievances, providing information, and making substitutions.

Direct mail A form of advertising in which a message is sent by mail to preselected targets.

Entrepreneur Someone who conceives of a product or service that fulfills a need in the marketplace.

Image The sum total of all the perceptions your customers and clients and all others have about you and your business.

Intern Student who works outside the university classroom for a grade and/or nominal fee. Arranged by the university and employers.

Leveraging The process of identifying and capitalizing on the smallest number of actions which produce the largest number of results.

Market The set of existing and prospective users of a product or service.

Marketing The process of planning and executing the conception, pricing, promotion, and distribution of ideas, goods, and services to create exchanges that satisfy individual and organizational objectives.

Marketing plan The hard-copy end-product of the marketing planning process.

Marketing research The systematic collection, analysis, and reporting of data to provide information for marketing decision making.

Marketing strategy The marketing logic by which a business seeks to achieve its marketing objectives.

Marketing vehicle That which is used in support of one's marketing plan and marketing strategies.

Market segment A distinct or definable subset of a target market.

Niche or **marketing niche** An identifiable market or market segment which can be readily and prosperously penetrated.

Personal selling A professional marketing effort involving face-to-face communication and feedback with the goal of making a sale or inducing a favorable attitude toward a company and its product or services.

Press or **news release** An announcement of community, state, national, or international interest distributed to media by the person or organization for and about whom the announcement is written.

Product differentiation Presenting a product so that it is perceived by customers as different from other products available.

Product line A group of products that are closely related because they satisfy a class of needs, are used together, or are sold to the same customers. Also can mean the range of products marketed by a company.

Professional service Businesses engaged in rendering advice, consultation, assistance, support, or specific results for a fee, usually on a retainer or hourly basis.

Promotion The act of furthering the growth and development of a business by generating exposure of goods or services to a target market.

Prospecting The activities involved in seeking potential buyers or customers; identifying and contacting likely candidates for purchase of your goods or services.

Reference A letter or testimony from a customer or client stating that your products and/or services were found to be of value.

Referral A name, provided to you by a customer, client, or other known party, of someone who has the potential to become a customer or client of your business or service.

Target market That portion of the total market that a company has selected to serve.

Telemarketing A systemized effort employing the telephone to develop new business, service existing accounts, or otherwise aid in the overall marketing process of a business.

Telephone script (or **telescript**) A written guide used in preparation for telephone contacts and making follow-up calls.

Trade association An organization established to benefit members of the same trade by informing them of issues and developments within the trade organization and about how changes outside the organization will affect them.

Vendor One who fulfills product or service needs.

SBA DISTRICT OFFICES

Alabama
2121 8th Avenue, North,
    Suite 200
Birmingham, AL 55403
205-731-1344

Alaska
222 West 8th Avenue,
    Room 67
Anchorage, AL 99513
907-271-4022

Arizona
2828 North Central Avenue,
    Suite 800
Phoenix, AZ 85004
602-640-2316

Arkansas
2120 Riverfront, Suite 100
Little Rock, AR 72202
501-324-5871

California
2719 North Air Drive,
    Suite 200
Fresno, CA 93727
209-487-5791

330 North Brand Boulevard,
    Suite 1200
Glendale, CA 91203
818-552-3210

660 J Street, Suite 215
Sacramento, CA 95814
916-498-6410

550 West C Street, Suite 500
San Diego, CA 92101
619-557-7250

455 Market Street, 6th Floor
San Francisco, CA 94104
415-744-6820

200 West Santa Ana Boulevard
Santa Ana, CA 92701
714-550-7420

Colorado
721 19th Street
Denver, CO 80202
303-844-3984

Connecticut
330 Main Street, 2nd Floor
Hartford, CT 06106
860-240-4700

Delaware
824 Market Street, Suite 610
Wilmington, DE 19801
302-573-6294

District of Columbia
1110 Vermont Avenue, NW,
    Suite 900
Washington, DC 20005
202-606-4000

Florida
1320 South Dixie Highway,
Suite 301
Coral Gables, FL 33146
305-536-5521

7825 Baymeadows Way,
Suite 100B
Jacksonville, FL 33256
904-443-1900

Georgia
1720 Peachtree Road, NW
6th Floor
Atlanta, GA 30369
404-347-2441

Guam
238 Archbishop F.C. Flores
Street, Room 508
Agana, GU 96910
671-472-7277

Hawaii
300 Ala Moana Boulevard
Honolulu, HI 96850
808-541-2990

Idaho
1020 Main Street, Suite 290
Boise, ID 83702
208-334-1696

Illinois
500 West Madison Street,
Suite 1250
Chicago, IL 60661
312-353-4528

511 West Capital Avenue,
Suite 302
Springfield, IL 62704
217-492-4416

Indiana
429 Pennsylvania Avenue,
Suite 100
Indianapolis, IN 46204
317-226-7272

Iowa
The Lattner Building
215 4th Avenue, SE, Suite 200
Cedar Rapids, IA 52401
319-362-6405

210 Walnut Street, Federal
Building, Room 749
Des Moines, IA 50309
515-284-4422

Kansas
100 East English Street
Wichita, KS 67202
316-269-6616

Kentucky
600 Dr. Martin Luther King,
Jr. Drive, Room 188
Louisville, KY 40202
502-582-5971

Louisiana
365 Canal Street, Suite 2250
New Orleans, LA 70130
504-589-6685

Maine
40 Western Avenue, Room 512
Augusta, ME 04330
207-622-8378

Maryland
10 S. Howard Street
Baltimore, MD 21202
410-962-4392

Massachusetts
10 Causeway Street,
   Room 265
Boston, MA 02222
617-565-5590

1441 Main Street, Suite 410
Springfield, MA 01103
413-785-0268

Michigan
477 Michigan Avenue,
   Room 515
Detroit, MI
313-226-6075

Minnesota
100 North 6th Street,
   Suite 610-C
Minneapolis, MN 55403
612-370-2324

Mississippi
2909 13th Street, Suite 203
Gulfport, MS 39501
601-863-4449

101 West Capitol Street,
   Suite 400
Jackson, MS 39201
601-965-4378

Missouri
323 West 8th Street, Suite 501
Kansas City, MO 64105
816-374-6708

815 Olive Street, Room 242
St. Louis, MO 63101
314-539-6600

620 South Glenstone,
   Suite 110
Springfield, MO 65802
417-864-7670

Montana
301 South Park, Room 334
Helene, MT 59626
406-441-1081

Nebraska
11145 Mill Valley Road
Omaha, NE 68154
402-221-4691

Nevada
301 East Stewart Avenue,
   Room 301
Las Vegas, NV 89125
702-388-6611

New Hampshire
Stewart Nelson Plaza, 143
    Main Street
Concord, NH 03301
603-225-1400

New Jersey
Two Gateway Center,
    4th Floor
Newark, NJ 07102
973-645-2434

New Mexico
526 Silver Avenue SW,
    Suite 312
Albuquerque, NM 87102
505-766-1870

New York
111 West Huron Street,
    Room 1311
Buffalo, NY 14202
716-551-4301

333 East Water Street
Elmira, NY 14901
607-734-8130

35 Pinelawn Road,
    Suite 207W
Melville, NY 11747
516-454-0750

26 Federal Plaza, Room 3100
New York, NY 10278
212-264-4354

100 State Street, Suite 410
Rochester, NY 14614
716-263-6700

401 South Salina Street,
    5th Floor
Syracuse, NY 13202
315-471-9393

North Carolina
200 North College Street,
    Suite A2015
Charlotte, NC 28202
704-344-6563

North Dakota
667 2nd Avenue North,
    Room 219
Fargo, ND 58102
701-239-5131

Ohio
525 Vine Street, Suite 870
Cincinnati, OH 45202
513-684-2814

11 Superior Avenue, Suite 630
Cleveland, OH 44114
216-522-4180

2 Nationwide Plaza,
    Suite 1400
Columbus, OH 43215
614-469-6860

Oklahoma
210 Park Avenue, Suite 1300
Oklahoma City, OK 73102
405-231-5521

Oregon
222 SW Columbia Street,
   Suite 500
Portland, OR 97201
503-326-2682

Pennsylvania
100 Chestnut Street, Suite 108
Harrisburg, PA 17101
717-782-3840

RBT Nix Building
900 Market Street, 5th Floor
Philadelphia, PA 19107
215-580-2722

Stegmaier Building
7 Wilkes-Barre Boulevard,
   Suite 407
Wilkes-Barre, PA 18702
717-826-6497

1000 Liberty Avenue
Federal Building, Room 1128
Pittsburgh, PA 15222
412-395-6560

Puerto Rico
Citibank Towers Place
252 Ponce de Leon Avenue
Hato Rey, PR 00918
787-766-5572

Rhode Island
380 Westminster Mall
Providence, RI 02903
401-528-4561

South Carolina
1835 Assembly Street,
   3rd Floor
Columbia, SC 29201
803-765-5377

South Dakota
110 South Phillips Avenue,
   Suite 201
Sioux Falls, SD 257102
605-330-4231

Tennessee
50 Vantage Way, Suite 201
Nashville, TN 37228
615-736-5881

Texas
606 North Carancahua,
   Suite 1200
Corpus Christi, TX 78476
512-888-3331

10737 Gateway West,
   Suite 320
El Paso, TX 79935
915-540-5586

4300 Amon Carter Boulevard,
   Suite 114
Fort Worth, TX 76155
817-885-6500

222 East Van Buren Street,
   Room 500
Harlingen, TX 78550
210-427-8533

9301 SW Freeway, Suite 550
Houston, TX 77074
713-773-6500

1611 Tenth Street, Suite 200
Lubbock, TX 79401
806-472-7462

727 East Durango,
   Room A527
San Antonio, TX 78206
210-472-5900

Utah
125 South State Street,
   Room 2237
Salt Lake City, UT 84138
801-524-5804

Virginia
1504 Santa Rosa Road
Dale Building, Suite 200
Richmond, VA 23229
804-771-2400

Vermont
87 State Street, Room 205
Montpelier, VT 05602
802-828-4422

U.S. Virgin Islands
3800 Crown Bay
V.I. Maritime Building
St. Thomas, VI 00802
787-774-8530

3013 Golden Rock
St. Croix, VI 00820
787-778-5380

Washington
1200 Sixth Avenue, Suite 1700
Seattle, WA 98101
206-553-7310

601 West 1st Avenue, 10th
   Floor East
Spokane, WA 99204
509-353-2810

Wisconsin
212 East Washington Avenue,
   Room 213
Madison, WI 53703
608-264-5261

310 West Wisconsin Avenue,
   Room 400
Milwaukee, WI 53203
414-297-3941

West Virginia
405 Capitol Street, Suite 412
Charleston, WV 25301
304-347-5220

168 West Street, 6th Floor
Clarksburg, WV 26301
304-623-5631

Wyoming
100 East B Street, Room 4001
Casper, WY 82602
307-261-6500

TAPPING INTO THE SMALL BUSINESS ADMINISTRATION (SBA)

SBA Answer Desk. A toll-free information center that answers questions about starting or running a business and how to get assistance. A telephone message system, the Answer Desk, is accessible 24 hours a day, seven days a week. Answer Desk operators are available Monday through Friday from 9 A.M. to 5 P.M. ET Call 800-8-ASK-SBA. To fax, dial 202-205-7064. For the hearing impaired, the TDD number is 704-344-6640.

SBA OnLine. An electronic bulletin board that provides concise and current information about programs and services that can assist in starting and running a business. It also includes many SBA publications. Accessed by modem (9600, n, 8,1), it operates 24 hours a day, seven days a week, and is updated daily. To access SBA OnLine, dial 800-697-4636 or 900-463-4636. The SBA OnLine number for the D.C, metro area is 202-401-9600.

On the Internet. The SBA Home Page [http://www.sba.gov] offers detailed information on SBA and other business services, access to SBA OnLine, and links to outside resources on the World Wide Web. The Web site will become a one-stop electronic link to business information and services the federal government provides. Users can download business forms and conduct many other business transactions. Also, visit the U.S. Business Advisor at: http://www.business.gov

Management Assistance Aids. The SBA produces and maintains a library of management-assistance publications and videos, which are available at nominal costs. A complete listing is available in the Resource Directory for Small Business Management.

BUSINESS COUNSELING AND TRAINING

Service Corps of Retired Executives (SCORE). Nationwide, 13,000 SCORE volunteers in nearly 400 chapters provide expert advice, based on their many years of firsthand experience and shared knowledge, on virtually every aspect of business. SCORE counselors are located at SBA field offices, business information centers, and some of SBAs small business development centers.

Small Business Development Centers (SBDCs). Funded and run by the SBA, SBDCs provide a variety of management and technical assistance to small businesses and would-be entrepreneurs. They are a cooperative effort among the SBA, the academic community, the private sector, and state and local governments.

Business Information Centers (BICs). Supported by its local SBA office, a BIC can assist you through access to state-of-the-art computer hardware and software and through counseling by SCORE volunteers. To find out if there is a BIC near you, call your SBA field office or access BIC locations by dialing SBA OnLine.

FURTHER READING

Adams, Bob, *Small Business Start-up*. Holbrook, MA: Adams Media, 1996.

Alessandra, Tony, *Charisma*. New York: Warner, 1998.

Alessandra, Tony, *The Platinum Rule*. New York: Warner, 1996.

Allen, S. Carol, *How to Successfully Run a Computer Bulletin Board for Profit*. Yucca Valley, CA: InfoLink, 1993.

Applegate, Jane, *201 Great Ideas for Small Business*. New York: Bloomberg Press, 1998.

Arnold, David, with Gail Rutman, *Business on the Internet: The Concise Handbook*. Eugene, OR: David Arnold & Associates, 1997.

Baber, Michael, *How Champions Sell*. New York: Amacom, 1997.

Bayan, Richard, *Words That Sell*. Westbury, NY: Asher-Gallant Press, 1984.

Bennett, Jarrett, *Making the Money Last*. Dubuque, IA: Kendall Hunt, 1996.

Brooks, Bill, *You're Working Too Hard to Make the Sale*. Burr Ridge, IL: Business One, Irwin, 1995.

Cialdini, Robert, *Influence: The Psychology of Modern Persuasion*, New York: New York: Quill, 1993.

Caples, John, *Tested Advertising Methods*, 4th ed. Englewood Cliffs, NJ: Prentice Hall, 1974.

Cathcart, Jim, *The Acorn Principle*. New York: St Martin's, 1998.

Connor, Richard, and Jeff Davidson, *Marketing Your Consulting & Professional Services*. New York: Wiley, 1997.

Davidson, Jeff, *Blow Your Own Horn: How to Market Your Career and Yourself*. Holbrook, MA: Adams Media, 1999.

Davidson, Jeff, *Breathing Space: Living & Working at a Comfortable Pace in a Sped-up Society*. Seattle: MasterMedia, 1999.

Davidson, Jeff, *The Complete Idiot's Guide to Reaching Your Goals*. New York: Macmillan, 1998.

Davidson, Jeff, The Joy of Simple Living. Emmaus, PA: Rodule, 1999.

Gershman, Michael. *Smarter Barter*. New York: Viking, 1986.

Godin, Seth, *eMarketing: Reaping Profits on the Information Highway*. New York: Perigee, 1995.

Gschwandtner, Gerhard, *How to Become a Master Sales Builder*. Englewood Cliffs, NJ: Prentice-Hall, 1987.

Haynes, Colin, *Paperless Publishing*. New York: McGraw-Hill, 1994.

Hedtke, John, *Using Computer Bulletin Boards*, 3rd ed. New York: MIS Press, 1995.

Hoge, Cecil, *The Electronic Marketing Manual: Integrating Electronic Media into Your Marketing Campaign*. New York: McGraw-Hill, 1993.

Hudgik, Steve, *Make Money Selling Your Shareware*. New York: McGraw-Hill, 1994.

Janal, Daniel, *Online Marketing Handbook:* New York: Van Nostrand Reinhold, 1995.

Negroponte, Nicholas, Ph.D., *Being Digital*. New York: Vintage, 1996.

Ott, Richard, *Creating Demand*. Burr Ridge, IL: Irwin, 1992.

Pagonis, General William G., *Moving Mountains*. Cambridge, MA: Harvard Business School Press, 1992.

Ries, Al and Jack Trout, *Positioning: The Battle for Your Mind*. New York: McGraw-Hill, 1981.

Schenot, Bob, *How to Sell your Software*. New York: John Wiley, 1994.

Woolf, Bob, *Friendly Persuasion*, New York: Putnam, 1990.

Yudkin, Marcia, *Six Steps to Free Publicity*. New York: Plume/ Penguin, 1994.

Yudkin, Marcia, *Marketing Online: Low Cost, High Yield Strategies for Small Businesses & Professionals*. New York: Plume, 1995.

Index

ABOUT THE AUTHOR

Jeff Davidson often is called to speak at conferences, conventions, and retreats and has made presentations to more than 500 groups in the United States, Europe, and Asia on topics related to excelling in an ever-changing environment, yet staying balanced and happy while confronting constant change. Comments such as "Best of the convention," or "Best we've ever heard" represent typical feedback to Jeff's presentations.

Jeff is the author of 25 books, more than 3,000 articles, and numerous audio and video tape programs. Jeff's book, *Marketing Your Consulting and Professional Services*, is considered to be one of the bibles in the field. Jeff's two-cassette album, *Get a Life* (Learn, Inc.), is a leading-edge program on living and working at a comfortable pace in a high-speed society. *The Joy of Simple Living* (Rodale) is one of the most comprehensive books in that genre.

Jeff's six-cassette album, *Simplifying Your Work and Your Life* (SkillPath), co-recorded with Dr. Tony Alessandra, gives career professionals the tools and practical information they need in the face of complexity in their everyday lives. Jeff and Tony's video (American Media Inc.) dramatically and humorously conveys the essence of the longer cassette version.

Jeff offers a blend of both keynote and seminar presentations on how to maintain balance while remaining profitable and competitive. Included among his presentations are:

- Breathing Space for Entrepreneurs
- Marketing in a Complex Environment
- Managing Multiple Priorities
- Handling Information Overload

Five of Jeff's speeches have been published in recent years in issues of the prestigious *Vital Speeches of the Day*, including "Relaxing at High Speed" "Choosing When It's Confusing," "Overworked or Overwhelmed?" "World Population and Your Life," and "Handling Information Overload," along side those of

Dr. Henry Kissinger, Lee Iacocca, William Bennett, Michael Eisner, and Alan Greenspan.

The *Washington Post*, where he's been featured eight times, called Jeff Davidson a "dynamo of business book writing." Millions of people have read about Jeff in *USA Today*, *Los Angeles Times*, *San Francisco Chronicle*, and the *Chicago Tribune*, or have seen him featured on "Good Morning America," "CBS Nightwatch," "CNBC," "Ask Washington," and hundreds of regionally based talk shows.

Jeff is one of a handful of distinguished authors who have had two or more of their books among "The Best Thirty Books of the Year" as selected by *Soundview Executive Book Summaries*. Other authors include Dr. Peter Drucker, Tom Peters, and Dr. Karl Albrecht. Cumulatively, Jeff's books have been selected by 20 major book clubs and published in 14 languages.

To inquire about Jeff's speaking availability, fax him at 919-932-9982, e-mail keynote@JeffDavidson.com, visit http://www.JeffDavidson.com, or call 919-932-1996.